MOSES AVALON'S

100

ANSWERS TO

50

QUESTIONS ON THE
MUSIC
BUSINE$$

D1361492

HAL•LEONARD®

Hal Leonard Books
An Imprint of Hal Leonard Corporation

Published in 2010 by Hal Leonard Books
An Imprint of Hal Leonard Corporation
7777 West Bluemound Road
Milwaukee, WI 53213

Trade Book Division Editorial Offices
33 Plymouth St., Montclair, NJ 07042

Printed in the United States of America

Book design by Adam Fulrath

Library of Congress Cataloging-in-Publication Data is available upon request.

ISBN 978-1-4234-8445-5

www.halleonard.com

To everyone who has
the courage to take the plunge,
the drive to divert rejection,
the talent to make a difference,
and the wisdom to know when to quit.

CONTENTS

INTRODUCTION

CAN I JUST GET ONE SIMPLE ANSWER? xi

How to Use This Book xiv

PART 1

I JUST JOINED A BAND/GROUP

QUESTIONS AND ANSWERS FOR THOSE GETTING STARTED 1

Introduction: It's the Simple Things 1

We're All Jammin', So Who Is the Songwriter? 2

What Is a Producer, and Why Do I Need One? 4

Touring: I'm a Studio Rat. Do I Really Need to Perform Live? 7

Can I Perform Live to a Prerecorded Track? 8

Do I Need to Learn to Read Music? 9

When Am I Really in the Band—for Good? 10

Do We Need to Incorporate or Trademark the Band/Group Name? 11

What Is a Copyright, and Do I Really Need One in the Internet Age? 14

How Do I Get a Copyright? 16

When Do I Need a Manager? 17

Are Fans Important in the Internet Age? 19

What Social Networks Are Worth Joining
to Get More Fans and Sell More Music? 21

How Can I Maintain an Efficient Mailing List That Works? 23

CONTENTS

How Do You Make Money from Music Other than Selling CDs? 29

What Do Major Labels Really Want from a New
Artist in Order to Sign Them?...32

Am I Too Old for a Record Deal? 34

What Music Biz Blogs Are Worth My Time? 34

Conclusion 39

PART 2

I JUST MADE MY FIRST LOUSY LITTLE DEAL

QUESTIONS AND ANSWERS FOR THOSE WHO HAVE GOTTEN SERIOUS 41

Introduction 41

Why Are All These Music Managers So Afraid/
Lazy About Signing New Artists? 42

What's a Good Deal, Anyway?...44

What Is a 360 Deal? How Is It Different from an "Old School" Deal,
and Do I Need to Sign Either to Be Successful?............................46

Does a 360 Deal Guarantee a Greater Commitment to the Artist?.................50

Why Are There So Many Scam Companies That Claim to Help
Indie Artists with Their Careers, and How Can I Avoid Them? 51

Are Music Conferences a Waste of Time?
Does Anyone Get Great Deals from Them?.....................................58

Are CDs Dead? When Will Digital Sales
Make Up the Majority of Revenue? 65

What Are the Pros and Cons of Working with a
Publishing Company? Should I Just Start My Own?........................68

Why the Heck Is Music Publishing So Arcane and
Hard to Explain to Anyone?...69

What Is a Good First Publishing Deal? 72

What's the Difference Between ASCAP, BMI,
and SESAC? Which One Should I Join? 73

Does Staying Indie Mean I'll Have More Freedom but Less Money?
Has Anyone Stayed Indie and Gone Platinum in the US?
How Did They Do It? 76

Does the Public Really Prefer Singles to Albums? 78

Why Don't Radio Stations Play Unsigned Acts?
Why Can't You Get on Radio Without Major Label Backing? 81

Where Should I Tour, and How Do I Get Booked? 83

Can You Get Discovered on the Internet, and
Will You Make Good Money Because People Hear You on YouTube? ... 84

How Much Can I Make If I Stay Indie? 85

How Much Money Do I Need to Invest
to Make It as an Artist or Producer? 86

What Kind of Terms Should Be in a Licensing Agreement? 89

Has the Internet Helped or Hurt the Music Business? 93

PART 3

I'M ABOUT TO SIGN MY FIRST REAL DEAL

QUESTIONS AND ANSWERS FOR THOSE WHO HAVE ARRIVED 97

Introduction 97

How Can I Tap into Money from Overseas? 99

What Are the Numbers: How Many Acts per Year
Do the Major Labels Sign and Release? 109

How Much Do the Majors/Indies Budget for Studio Recordings? 113

How Much Do the Majors/Indies Budget for Tour Support? 116

What Is "Payola"? Why Is It Important? Will It Ever Stop? 123

Do I Need a Written Business Plan? How Do I Do It? 128

CONTENTS

PART 4

I WANT OUT OF THIS DEAL

QUESTIONS AND ANSWERS FOR THOSE WHO HAVE HAD ENOUGH 133

Introduction: They Never Said It Would Be Easy,
but They Did Say It Would Be Fun 133

With Digital Technology It Is Possible to Track Almost All
Performances. So Why Are the Societies Not Collecting
or Paying the Royalties Due Their Independent Artists? 134

Why Do the U.S.-Based PROs Persist in Their Archaic
and Inaccurate Method of Monitoring? 134

Can I Just Stop Making Music Once I'm Signed? 140

Why Doesn't the Government Do Something About Piracy? 145

I'm Being Hassled About Song Theft. What Can I Do? 149

How Can I Stop Some Scab P2P Site from
Distributing or BitTorrenting My Music? 152

Reversion of Master Rights: When Is an Artist Eligible? 153

Should I Let My Record Company Keep the Rights
After They Revert to Me? 158

PART 5

WILL THINGS EVER CHANGE?

QUESTIONS AND ANSWERS FROM VETERANS ABOUT
THE STATE OF THE INDUSTRY 161

Will They? 161

With So Much Music Being Given Away, How Can a
Producer Make Money in the Coming Years? 162

Why Has the Average Music Lover Happily
Given Up Their CD Audio Quality for a Lousy MP3? 164

Why Were Major Labels So Slow/Resistant to
Respond to the Internet as a Sales Platform in the Early 2000s? 168

With CD Sales Going into the Abyss,
How Are Major Labels Staying in Business?...182

Will the Music Business Survive Another 20 Years?...............................186

AFTERWORD

WHAT IS THE MUSIC BIZ FOR?

Is It Just for Making Money, or Can It Really
Be a Vehicle for Social Change? Is There Anything to the 60's Idea
That We Can Organize for Change Through Popular Music? 195

APPENDIX

APPENDIX..201

Complete List of Foreign Performing Rights Organizations........................201

Major Label Organization and Goals...203

Passive Revenue Streams in the Music Business 204

ACKNOWLEDGMENTS

ACKNOWLEDGMENTS 205

INTRODUCTION

Can I Just Get One Simple Answer?

Are you satisfied with the level of success you've achieved with your music career? Or do you need a bit of coaching?

Every time I lecture, I set aside time for an extended Q&A period. It's become expected, and many who come to hear me speak do so more for the opportunity to get some free consulting from "The Music Business Expert" than to hear my take on some recent development. I'm happy to do it and feel honored that so many value my advice.

It never fails, however, that within a catalog of some really intelligent questions will be two that I dread and which never fail to surface:

"Dr. Avalon . . ." (it's an honorary title—I'm not even a college graduate) ". . . how do I get a record deal?"

I sigh. This is a stupid question, and everyone in the audience knows it. They shift in their seats, getting ready for me to hand this person their head. But I'm required out of sheer professionalism to answer it with patience. And the answer goes like this:

"Well, first of all, are you sure you even want one?"

The person nods, and I continue, "Okay, start by making great music, then get out there and really sell it hard. Tour, make fans, sell merch. Eventually, if you're doing everything right, a label or some deep pocket will notice you and offer you a contract. Hopefully one you can make money from. That's the simple soundbite answer."

The audience releases their breath for two reasons. One, they are all mostly doing those things already, so I didn't shock them with something they have missed; and two, I answered the question quickly, without taking precious time away from more important questions. But what happens next (and you'd be surprised how often) is that the next person I call on whose hand is raised will ask the other question I hate: "Dr. Avalon, how do *I* get a record deal?"

And now I'm ready to throw something.

So, let me save you some time if you're considering buying this book to answer that question: That question is not answered any better in the next 200 pages than it is in the paragraph above. However, in some ways this entire book is one big answer to the smaller sub-processes that go behind that question. Everybody wants a deal of some kind; one with respectable numbers. But how do you get there? What do you do after you get it? We can all presume the basics, but what about the nuances? And that brings us, if not to the answer, to the reason for this book's existence.

Everybody needs a coach. It doesn't matter what field you're in, or what hobby you take up. We are not born with expert knowledge of everything, nor are we designed to be able to give ourselves a haircut, so to speak. We need mentors. Someone to turn to when the going gets tough, or even for the simple day-to-day reassurance that we're making the right move.

This book is my response. *100 Answers to 50 Questions About the Music Business: A Troubleshooting Manual to Improve Music Business Excellence*. I know that there are some people who will turn to the Table of Contents to count them. They want to make sure that if they're going to pay for a book that advertises answers to 50 questions, that they are all there. I'll save you some time again: There are far more than 50 questions answered in this book. I'd guess that over 200 questions are answered. So why two (or more) answers for each? That is my homage to the Zen concept that there is rarely a single correct answer to any meaningful question. Like a river, answers flow in a direction that takes us on a journey. A single point of view is the product of a narrow mind, and in his or her search for clarity the traveler cannot afford rigidity.

And so, this book is more than just answers. It is your music business coach. Keep it handy for when you need advice.

Any book that attempts to combine or condense wisdom into a usable digest may have one editor, but it has to have many contributors. In a very real way, I am only the co-author of this book. I wrote the answers, but you, my readers, wrote the questions. There are over 14,000 of you on my personal mailing list, and through the RSS feed on **www.mosesavalon.com**, I would estimate that there are just south of 100,000 of you in total. When I e-mailed my readers and asked them what they wanted me to answer in my next book, they wrote in with questions. I picked the most frequent ones, the most interesting ones, and the ones I thought I could answer in meaningful yet uncommon ways, and here they are. (Oddly enough, the "How do I get a record deal" question did not surface.)

I know some of you will be saying, "But where is my question?" It's here. I promise. But it may not be in exactly in a form you recognize. I frequently amalgamated similar questions, or grouped them into a subchapter dealing with the general topic, like ASCAP, 360 Deals, and publishing. Sometimes questions are answered in my other books and were not appropriate for this forum.

So first, I want to thank all of you for your contributions. This is very much a book by and for the people.

I've written several books and hundreds of articles about the music biz, but none with this simple approach. Many books are targeted toward either beginners or experts, or the creative side versus the business side. This book is designed to help everyone. The secret and unique approach to this book's format is based on a new science and teaching aide called *heuristics*. This is a very hard word to define, but basically it means learning by building off of existing knowledge rather than teaching something from the ground up. Here's a quick example.

You read a sentence that goes, "This situation was so morally complex even Washington would have trouble keeping a straight face."

You scratch your head and wonder, "What does that mean? I know who Washington was, but what was it about Washington that would apply to this?" So you try to look up info on "Washington." In the old format of teaching (the "algorithmic" or "Socratic" methods) you'd get something like this:

"George Washington was a plantation owner and military general in the first 13 American colonies. He was a general in the Revolutionary War and became the first president of the United States. He was most known for being honest, because he destroyed a *Prunus alabamensis*, and when confronted by his father, he confessed to the deed."

There is lots of information here that may be very useful, but only one small piece is applicable to you. Plus, you probably already know the other stuff. So you only learned what you already knew. Who has time for that?

Heuristic way: You look up Washington in a book and find "Washington, George: first US president; confessed to his father that he cut down a valuable tree, proving his honesty."

Short and to the point. You can fill in the blanks and connect the dots yourself. This saves you lots of time, but it also allows a single book to cover a wide range of topics.

This is a very oversimplified example of heuristics, and one that I'm sure will have academics pounding their fists on the table in frustration. Academics love details and lots of complex, long answers. But as teachers of the music business, this book can be used to guide their lessons and act as a launching point for debate over important issues without making students read long and excessively didactic books on music business theory. Theories are for scientists doing things in the controlled environment of a lab. We live in the real world. We need answers now and fast, with a minimal amount of fluff. And let's be honest: the music business can hardly be called a controlled environment.

As far as finding easy-to-understand, ready-to-apply answers to questions on the business of music is concerned, you are holding your only salvation. I give you my word: Ain't nothing out there that will boil it down like this book will. And where this book falls short, I'll tell you where you can find more involved answers, saving you more time and money on your road toward music business excellence and success.

How to Use This Book

This is not the type of book that you buy and stick on a shelf or loan to a buddy, never to be seen again. It's the kind you keep handy and consult whenever you get stuck. Which, if you're like many of us, is several times a year. This book will be a companion to you for life. Treat it like a life partner, with respect, and in return it will give you years of service. Don't put it where you'll forget about it in a move, or worse yet, give it away to someone whom you think really needs to read it. Let them make their own investment in their education. They will appreciate it more.

This book's sections are mutually interdependent. That means that even though there is a common theme that builds upon previous chapters, each section is self-contained and can be read independently of the rest of the book. There is no "starting point." But since the publisher makes me put numbers on each page, we do need to have some order, so I've organized the book according to status. In other words, where you are in your career. You can see by the title of each chapter if the level of an answer is going to give you what you need. Sometimes similar questions pop up in different chapters of the book. But you'll see that there are very different answers in each chapter. That's because the answer I'd give someone starting their career is very different from the answer I'd give to a veteran.

Browse around and have fun with this book. Its knowledge is for use. Share it and let others know if you agree or disagree with it. Discussion is the root of our freedom and the key to gaining higher understanding of any subject. Don't let anyone tell you you're wrong for believing something just because it makes no sense to them. Sometimes the right answer is counterintuitive. Often, in fact, that is the case with the business of music. And what seems simple on the surface is more complex when you drill down. Explore and be open to learning opinions that you will not find in the common chat rooms or on Facebook. This is your Kabala, your Rosetta Stone. You're holding it. Begin to learn its secrets by turning the page.

—Moses Avalon

I Just Joined a Band/ Group

Questions and Answers for Those Getting Started

Introduction: It's the Simple Things

So you just played your first gig, got your rehearsal shut down because of a noise complaint, or fell in love with the idea of making music a way of life. Welcome to an insane world that is maddening, litigious, libidinous, frustrating, and the best damn time you ever had earning a (tough) living. The music space offers it all. It doesn't matter if your style is rock, rap, hip-hop, Latin, or pop. Every aspect of making music is a roller-coaster ride filled with emotional extremes.

In this chapter I'm going to answer the most common questions confronting someone just starting out in his or her musical career. Some of these answers might seem too simple, but there is beauty in a simple answer. As you move through this book you'll see the answers become more and more complex—even answers to the same or similar questions asked in the first part of the book. Why is that? Well, as your career progresses, the answer to a particular question gets more complex. It's morally wrong to bombard a person with a complex answer early on in their career. Artists need encouragement, not intellectual roadblocks. There is always time for the short-haired, legally correct answers later, when there is more at stake.

If you don't see a question or answer relating to something that you're dealing with, you can always e-mail me or check the archives on my website: www.MosesAvalon.com.

I answer all my own e-mail. You can also reach me through Facebook or Twitter: @mosesavalon.

We're All Jammin', So Who Is the Songwriter?

Sounds like a simple question to answer, right? Think again. More disputes in the music space are about who wrote what than just about anything else. When everyone is jamming in the same room it becomes hard to remember who wrote what. Well, not to worry—the law makes it real easy.

The reason for the confusion is that despite the fact that we have a very detailed Copyright Act that explains the rights of an author, nowhere in that Act are the words "song," "jam," or "track" defined. The closest word we have is "composition," and that's the word used in the trade when discussing what most would call a "song," track," or "jam" but . . .

But a composition is not a "track." A track would be a *recording* of a composition. And a composition would not be "beats" or a jam. Those are musical *arrangements* of the composition. Legally, the composition (or song) is composed of only two combined things: the lyrics and the melody. The melody is a single line of musical notes that guides the lyrics.

So let's say that you wrote a rap, and then your friend joined together a few samples to make a beat, or your guitar player buddy came up with a chord progression that sounds really slammin'. You then sing or rap over it. Poof—you have your first hit. But who wrote it?

Your friend may think that because he came up with the instrumentation that he is at least the co-writer of the composition. But unless his lick is part of the melody that follows the lyrics, he would be wrong. Legally, you and you alone wrote that song, since you wrote the lyrics and came up with the part that people will sing when they sing those lyrics.

I'll bet you're already saying, "Dang! Good thing I bought this book." But there is more to this. First, your "melody" had better be original, meaning it better not be too much like anyone else's. That's not so easy to do, since pop songwriters have been cranking out thousands of copyrighted songs since 1907. And believe it or not, if your melody is too much like one of their songs you could get in a bit of trouble if you knew about it and decided to use it in your recording without permission. But don't worry about that just yet. No one that I know of has ever sued an unknown songwriter for borrowing a melody to record a few demos. In fact, you probably won't hear from any lawyers unless the melody you accidentally stole is a hit in its own right. The odds of that are not worth contemplating at this stage. Have fun for now and steal anything you want while you're developing your personal style. Shakespeare did it and so did your favorite songwriter—fact. The important thing to grasp here is that guitar riffs, drum beats, and music grooves are *not* considered part of the song—legally.

Big But

However, to avoid tension, it's become industry standard to split the credit for writing the music with those in your group who inspired your melody. It's a good standard too, as it keeps everyone feeling cool and keeps productive partnerships moving in the right direction. Don't get greedy. If the song's a hit there will be plenty of cash to go around.

How Do I Know That the Person I'm Sending My Demo to Won't Steal My Song?

You can't, really. The chapter in my first book, *Confessions of a Record Producer,* called "The Myth of Copyright Protection" shows that even with money and fame there's no guarantee of security. And the law will only protect those who have the cash to take people to court. However, there is some solace. It's very risky to rip people off. It can end up bankrupting you if you get caught. So ask yourself a key question: do the people you're sending your music to seem like the kind of people who would care if they went bankrupt? If they seem to really care about music, your work, and having a relationship with you, then it's a safe bet.

What Is a Producer, and Why Do I Need One?

This is another one of those questions that seems obvious on the surface, but is in fact more complex than most people starting out realize. I suppose you could say that the producer is the person who gets the "producer's credit." And you would be about as close to creating an accurate definition as anyone.

In practicality, the producer is like the director on a movie: he or she works with the talent to mold the sound of the recordings. But the producer technically can also just be the person who pays for the recording, since generally the person who pays often has final say over the decisions that go into the recording, although not always.

In the pro world the producer is responsible for completing

the project on time and on budget. He or she signs a contract that ensures that the project will be delivered per the terms of the recording contract. This often implies that the producer is in the creative driver's seat, but this is not necessarily the case all the time. Regardless, if the project is turned in late, it's the producer's fault. If it sounds bad, we blame him too, unless circumstances made it hard to complete the job.

As you start your career, you will likely be your own producer. You will book the sessions, decide what takes are keepers, and oversee the mix, mastering and delivering the song(s) to the plant or digital store. But as you move into the pro arena, you may want to work with someone who can bring things to the project that you can't: a better studio, better talent, a certain sound that you want. Although you may still be making many creative decisions, don't forget that what distinguishes a producer from a co-producer or the artist is the concept of *responsibility*. You may be putting in all the hours in the studio, but if someone else is legally or financially responsible for the delivery of the project, that person is the producer. Show them respect.

The Basics of Getting Started in Music

So you want to be a record producer? I have some foolproof advice.

The four points below may seem to be too simple on the surface, but 20 years of great experience and advice are encoded within their simplicity. Read these steps carefully and apply them. If you follow these four steps you will have eliminated many of the barriers to success. The rest will come from persistence, talent, and a bit of luck.

1. Have a great demo. You need a demo for your material. If you're an artist, it should be material that you have written or co-written. (Or, if you are a producer, something that you have produced entirely.)

Several points of order:

a. Avoid cover songs. Let me say it again: Avoid cover songs. Cover songs show off other people's talent. (Don't use them unless your new version is radically different from the original. And I hesitate to even offer that caveat, because you'll brainwash yourself into thinking that yours is sufficiently different. It's probably not. Just avoid putting cover songs on your demo.)

b. Your songs should be well recorded. This does not necessarily mean expensively recorded.

c. Do not copy the style of several other artists. Your demo should represent a specific genre (i.e., R&B, rock, hip-hop, rap, trance, country) and not show off how many different styles you can imitate perfectly. Record companies hate this. It shows them that you have no direction.

2. Contact people who "shop" material to labels, artists, and publishers. Speak to individuals with a track record in this area. Lawyers are a common stop for this, as are managers or "shoppers," as the term has more recently evolved. All of these people will want a contract. This is normal, but don't sign anything without consulting someone you trust. (I offer very cheap consultations for unsigned artists when you get to this stage. Go to www.mosesavalon.com and send me an e-mail.)

3. Avoid "wannabes" who will tell you that they can give your demo to someone "important," but it must go through them. This makes them your agent, and can get complicated. If they really want to help you, explain that to them and ask them to make the introduction to the "important" person and let you or your real representative present the demo. If they have a problem with you representing yourself, they are probably full of crap. However, you must use your judgment. Today's wannabe can sometimes turn out to be tomorrow's executive. (In Confessions of a Record Producer I have a checklist to use to see if the person you're dealing with is a control freak or for real.)

4. Don't give up. Thomas Edison tried and failed hundreds of times to invent the light bulb before he succeeded. The Beatles were turned down by many major labels before getting signed. Persistence + talent = luck.

Touring: I'm a Studio Rat. Do I Really Need to Perform Live?

No.

The answer to this question before the year 2005 was "yes." But the Internet has created careers in music that were never before possible. Now you don't have to just be one artist. You can be several. You can have a rock band, a hip-hop act, and be a studio rat whose public never sees his face.

Having said that, let's reword the question: Does touring help sell records?

Yes.

People want to connect with the artists they like. Sure, if you're doing a one-off recording with no real image—like a novelty record, or dance groove—you can get away with not touring, and even have a hit. But building a following over time, one that will buy just about anything you put out, almost without exception requires some public face time. For this, touring is the way to go.

Many bloggers like to say that for a modern music career, selling records is over, and claim that you make most of your money by touring. I disagree. In fact, it's the opposite. Touring makes sense if you're U2 or Eminem. But if you're unknown, no one is going to pay to see you anyway. Plus, even big acts still make most of their money off of the sales of their recorded music. Eventually they will be too old to tour, but their music will live on in movies, TV shows, commercials, websites, and albums. Touring is an important building block to create that revenue stream. But it's an expensive one. Tours cost big money to launch, and often just break even. (See the section on touring, page 116.)

So once you have momentum, you'll want to stop putting that money (and yourself) at risk with road trips. If you've planned your career correctly, it's the sale of the master recordings that will put more coin in your pocket over the 20-year span of a music career.

Can I Perform Live to a Prerecorded Track?

Why not? Everyone else does. Whenever you see an artist jumping around on stage, there is a better than 80 percent chance that they are lip-syncing at least some parts of the performance. Why? Because a great vocal performance is hard to deliver when you're standing still, let alone dancing and doing flips on stage under 90-degree lights wearing uncomfortable costumes.

Everyone fakes it live. There are exceptions—artists known more for their vocal ability than their dance moves, for example. These artists will sit and sing at the piano, or on a stool while they strum their guitar.

Want to dare to sing live on national television? I got two

words for you—Taylor Swift. Google her performance at the 2010 Grammys. It was horrendous and embarrassed her team. Did it hurt her career? Hard to say, but I don't think she'll be making that mistake again.

What if you get caught? No biggie. Believe me, it's better to be caught lip-syncing than to deliver a bad performance and have everyone talking about it for a decade. Most people understand the challenges of a live show and don't expect it to be perfect. Some will argue that this means you can get away with a mediocre live performance. I would argue the opposite. Technology has conditioned people to expect a great live performance. Give it to them. If singing to a track makes things easier for you, do it.

Do I Need to Learn to Read Music?

It can't hurt.

Many great artists never learned to read music. Paul McCartney of the Beatles could not read a note, and only eventually taught himself to read music well after he was an established superstar.

If you want to be an artist or songwriter, reading music is certainly optional, by the odds. But if you want to have a career as a musician, then it takes on a greater priority. Almost all studio gigs require that you at least be able to read a "lead chart"—a sheet with chord progressions. If you're playing bass, piano, or just about anything except guitar, you have to be able to read the bass lines and chord voicings in order to improvise your part easily, and without wasting expensive studio time. If you're a vocalist, you MUST be able to sight-read. Vocalists tend to make three times the wage of most instrumentalists in commercial sessions, so it's worth it to lean this valuable skill. Also, for instrumentalists, session playing and pit orchestra work is the backbone of most people who make a living in music, so if you can, learn to read music. You'll be thankful later.

When Am I Really in the Band—for Good?

Simple answer: never. Ever see the movie *Rock Star* with Mark Wahlberg? It's not an entirely unrealistic story. You could be touring with a band and have made six platinum albums with them, and then one day a lawyer shows up and says, "You're out."

How is that possible? Well, at the amateur level there is no such thing as a band as a legal entity. It's just a bunch of friends hanging out together and playing. But as soon as they start writing songs together (see the question, "We're All Jammin', So Who Is the Songwriter?" for more on that), then they've entered into a partnership, even though they didn't sign any paperwork. Now you have a co-writing team. One that plays out together, creates property together, and performs under a name.

But are you secure if you're, say, the drummer? If you're the singer, maybe, because you're the face of the band, but if you're a drummer or other instrumentalist, you are quite replaceable.

As a band becomes more popular and decides to go pro, it typically enters into a "partnership agreement." This contract, prepared by a lawyer, is designed to give each member some security. Each member gets stock in the "company." The company is the band as embodied in the partnership agreement. So let's say that there are five players in the group: a singer/keyboardist, DJ, drummer, bass player, and backup singer/guitarist.

Each player would get 20% of the stock in a company called "The Band, Inc."

After this agreement is signed, if the band wanted to get rid of the DJ because he's not showing up for rehearsals, they'd have to buy him out of his position. What is that worth? It depends on how much money you're making as a band—not at your day job that supports the band. If you're making zero, you can probably give him a dollar. But if the DJ can get three other members to vote to keep him "in" even though he's not showing up, that's

80% of the vote and then you're stuck giving him 20% of everything, even if he doesn't show up. Sound silly? Maybe, but this is how it's done.

This is why I don't recommend entering into a partnership agreements until a label wants to sign you, or you're making real money as a band, or you have a very big sponsor (oftentimes your parents, to start out). You never know who you're going to need to replace.

Do We Need to Incorporate or Trademark the Band/ Group Name?

Trademarking

If ever there was a colossal waste of time for someone starting out, it's this. Lawyers are fond of scaring anyone who will listen into filing for a trademark for their band's name, because that is how they make money.

Without directly disagreeing with the legal community (which routinely charges $1,000 and up to file these trademarks for you), I have a somewhat different take on it. First, the stock answer: If an artist is serious about a long-term career and branding the band's name so that they can make money off of it—and also to keep others from ripping them off—it is advisable to trademark the name at the earliest possible stage to lock it down so that the band exclusively owns it worldwide—before someone else does.

Then there is the other way (my way) to think about it: trademarking is largely a "squatter's" world. Whoever makes their name the most known in the shortest amount of time usually wins the dispute over a trade name. The fact that you were born with a particular name makes no difference whatsoever, and will not even be relevant in most court cases where these conflicts are resolved. However, operating under that name for some time is *very* relevant: selling product under the band name; playing out; maintaining a website, and serving downloads to fans.

Is it important to trademark a band name eventually? Yes! When you go pro. What lawyers will rarely tell you is that after you spend the money to trademark your name, you are obligated to sue anyone else who tries to squat on it. If you don't, then you lose your trademark—forever.

So, let's say that you spend some cash on a trademark and now you're gigging out, playing the local clubs, and low and behold, some other group is gigging under the exact same name. They don't have a trademark, so naturally you believe you can ask them to stop playing out under that name. Well, you can ask, but if they don't listen, you will have to take them to court. If you can't afford that (which will cost anywhere from $2,500 to $25,000), then you cannot stop them. If you cannot stop them legally, you have forfeited the right to have that name as a trademark. Now you've wasted the $1,000 it cost you to trademark your name. Why don't lawyers tell you this? Well, they know that you won't bother to do it until it makes financial sense. They also make money both ways: registering the mark and then defending it.

My take: Since labels or other benefactors will often pay for trademarking when you sign with them, you don't need to go to the expense yourself when you are just a garage band. Save your money. Do a "poor man's" trademark instead when you're just starting out: Establish a URL with your band or act's name in it; get bookings under that name, and make sure there is no confusion in your region (remember that trademarks go by region—it's okay if there is another band in another state with the same name); sell stuff with your act's name on it; keep the receipts.

Here's a little secret that few people know about: You can put the little "TM" next to your name without actually having an official trademark from the state. Since most people do not know that this mark has little legal weight, it sometimes acts as a deterrent. Or here's a tip from veteran music lawyer Ben McLane: Just to be safe, you can "reserve" the name with the trademark office if you intend to use it, and follow up with proof later once you have started playing gigs, etc. Make it official by going to www.uspto.gov and applying online. It's worth the time and money to avoid name disputes/hassles down the line.

Incorporating

The same goes for incorporating. Don't bother until you go pro. Corporations are for protecting assets like your house or your savings from other writers or bands suing you for copyright infringement or injuries—like if your roadie falls off a van while you're on tour.

But, I'm willing to bet that if you're reading this chapter, you probably don't own a house or have much in the way of savings—yet. When you do, and when a good portion of your money is coming from music, it's time to incorporate.

A far cheaper thing to do to pave the way for a future incorporation is something called a DBA ("Doing Business As"). This is a cheap business license that most county clerks can issue you for a few bucks. You might want to get this if you're thinking about opening up a bank account in your group's name. It's a small gesture that makes you look more professional, and will ultimately make industry folks take you more seriously. Cost: about $150, if done with a service. (Use a service. The paperwork is nasty.)

What Is a Copyright, and Do I Really Need One in the Internet Age?

There are three answers to this: Short, long, and complete. Short answer: Now more than ever. The longer answer I'll give in a minute. The complete answer would be a book unto itself. (Several, really. And several have already been written.)

The long beginner answer is as follows: First off, what is a copyright? There are many complex answers involving bundles of rights and constitutional issues of monopoly. But none of those matter for now. Very simply, a copyright is the right to make a copy. Meaning that if you own a creative work and you created it, you and you alone get to decide who makes copies of it. That means all copies, including new versions of your work and performances of the work. So if you wrote a song and it's well known and someone wants to change the lyrics, they have to get your permission before they can profit off of their new version (called a "derivative work" in legal mumbo-jumbo). If someone wants to perform your song in public and you have not published it already (like put it on a CD or made it available for a download), they need your permission as well.

So why is this more important than ever in the Internet age? Well, if you're asking this question, it's probably because you've been inundated with propaganda from Internet Service Providers (ISPs) about "information wanting to be free," and other such slogans. This was born out of the lawsuits that tried to stop P2P file sharing of music in the early to mid-2000s.

ISPs love the idea that users can share music without paying for it. It promotes the use of their services, which makes them money. About $130 million a year, according to some experts. But it happens to be illegal, and, depending on your views on the ownership of creative works, immoral as well. So to make the public feel better about enabling it to commit nefarious acts, they concocted the slogan and campaign that "information wants to be free."

Google and Apple love these types of slogans, until it means that their patents and trade secrets will also be free. Then they are willing to sue and initiate arrests to protect their property.

Copyrights, along with patents and trade secrets, are all part of a body of law called "intellectual property." This is exactly like owning a house or a car, except that this property is "idea" driven. The concept is simple: The inventor or creator of a new idea gets to have absolute control of their creation for a period of time, after which it becomes the property of the general public. When this happens, the creation is called "public domain."

Until a creation is public domain, the author/creator gets to profit from it and decide who gets to make copies or versions of the idea. For patents the time limit is 14 years, with one 14-year renewal. For songs it's the life of the author plus 35 years with one 35-year renewal, or a flat 95 years, depending on certain circumstances.

Sounds simple, right?

While the idea that copyrights are meaningless is currently in vogue in chat rooms, rest assured that this is not going to last. Eventually copyrights for music will be back to where they had been prior to the Internet age. How do I know this? Well, intellectual property rights are the foundation of almost all commerce in the US. They affect not only record companies wanting to protect their music catalogues, but also airplane blueprints and military secrets, as well as trade secrets, such as the recipe for Coca-Cola.

All of these things are protected under one form of intellectual property law or another.

The erosion of those laws is beginning with music and copyright, but this is only the outer sphere. Eventually this trend could work its way into patents and military secrets.

If record companies lose legal ground, the next target of the "information wants to be free" movement will certainly be the trade secrets that affect thousands of American companies. Including ISPs.

ISPs know this. They know that the battle to protect unique ideas will never reach their front door, because there are too many companies that would fall apart if information and trade secrets were truly "free." So their "information is free" campaign is not only disingenuous, but because even ISPs know that this is a bogus argument, it also makes a fool out of anyone who supports it. As companies who want to profit off of a piece of music, they are logically compelled to reject this concept of "free information," even if they may agree with it morally. It's simply in conflict with making money off of art.

Because so much of the economy of the US (and of the West in general) is built around the ownership of ideas, in all likelihood copyrights will become even more valuable in the future.

How Do I Get a Copyright?

According to urban legend, all you have to do is send something to yourself in the mail and you've protected it. Wrong. You need a federal ID number from the Library of Congress in order to seriously protect your work. It used to be a bit difficult to get that, because you had to fill out certain forms. But now the Library has modernized. You can register online, and it only takes a few minutes to fill out the form and attach an MP3 to your request.

Don't hesitate to do this. Do it the moment you have finished a version of your song that you consider to be releasable. It's the best $30 you'll ever spend on yourself: Go to www.copyright.gov.

PA or SR—Which Form Do I Use?

If you're safety conscious, both. The SR stands for "sound recording." This will protect the recording of your song. If you've worked a long time on the production, this will ensure that no one makes copies without your permission. Form PA ("performing arts") will protect the underlying composition, or "the song," which is the lyrics and the melody.

Each form costs $35 (that's one form for each song and one form for each recording of each song, or $70 per song) if you use the Copyright Office's fancy new online registration system.

What most people do to save a lot of bread (and I'm not recommending this) is use the SR form to register a bunch of songs as a "collection" of work. This way they spend only $35 to have several songs "registered."

There are downsides to this, but they are minor compared to not registering your material *at all*, and besides that, it's becoming standard practice despite the downside potential, unless you are a record company or publishing company, in which case you would do two forms (PA and SR) for each track.

For more information, I recommend the Copyright Office's own website (www.copyright.gov). They have a pretty good Q&A search engine and a nifty downloadable movie on how to register your stuff right from where you sit. There's also a bunch of links on my website, **www.mosesavalon.com**, under "Artist's Resources ."

When Do I Need a Manager?

Simple answer: Almost never, unless you are almost famous.

What exactly do managers do, and how valuable are they in the grand scheme of things? This is complicated, because managers seem to come from every corner of the music business. Let's say you're a recording artist (or hope to become one) and you're looking for a manager. What will he or she do for the 15 to 20 percent that they will take off the top of your gross earnings?

→Managers shop and negotiate the deal between the artist and the record label. *But wait—doesn't a lawyer do that?* Well, yes.

→Managers make sure that the artist gets their proper royalty payments. *But wait, wait—doesn't an accountant or business manager do that?* Well, yes.

➜Managers help the artist select material for the record and help develop the sound. *But wait—doesn't the producer do that?* Well, yes.

➜Managers supervise the artist's interviews and press releases, and make sure that nothing too negative leaks to the press (unless they want it to). *But doesn't a publicist do that?* Most definitely.

➜Managers help mold the artist, such as giving them the proper look. *But can't you get a stylist or image consultant to do that for a few bucks?* Sure.

➜Managers oversee the construction and optimization of the artist's Web presence. *But can't you get a webmaster and viral marketing person to do that for a monthly fee*? Yep.

Give up? This call and answer may, on the surface, seem like I'm down on managers, but I'm not. A manager is a classic example of the whole being greater than the sum of its parts. Each of a manager's functions could be delegated to one of the other pros. But a manager has his or her hands in all of these areas and, if he or she is a good one, keeps the machinery oiled with funny stories, rounds of drinks, free tickets, and the three "R's" of the record industry— relationships, relationships, relationships. The best way to think about a manager is like a toll booth. You could bypass them and take a longer road to get to where you want to go. But if you want to get there faster and safer on a nice, paved interstate highway, you have to pay the 20 percent toll. Good managers keep everyone talking to each other. They are master schmoozers, and because there are only two qualifications for the profession—1) that they be good talkers; and 2) that they have lots of contacts—many people from many backgrounds call themselves managers. Here's my definition of a good manager: "Someone who pays attention to *how* things get done, as opposed to *what* gets done."

But when do you need one? Simple answer: when you cannot handle the above list on your own. Now, notice I didn't say, "don't *want* to"; I said "cannot." There's a big difference. Sure, everyone *wants* a maid. I hate picking up my socks in the morning. But I don't pay someone 20 percent of my income to do it.

If you're still playing in the garage and booking local clubs, chances are that your "manager" is a friend who wants to be involved with your group. Nothing wrong with that, just don't sign a contract with him or her. Give them something that shows you're appreciative, without a long-term commitment. Wait until you get an offer from a label, production company, or sponsor.

One exception: there are a few managers that are so big that they are de facto labels. If one of them approaches you, call me. (See the other question on managers, page 42.) I'll find you a great lawyer to help. Never, ever say yes or no without consulting someone first.

Are Fans Important in the Internet Age?

Yeah, but probably in a different way than before. Hits in the near future will likely not be made by a marketing campaign leading to album sales and snowballing, like in the old days. The progression will more likely be like this:

A track gets placed in a goofy YouTube upload. People learn about it through social networks and e-mail and forward the link to their friends, some of whom go to the artist's website to download it, share it, etc. Eventually, film and TV producers license the track for a movie or show, which leads to more downloads, etc.

It's a viral effect. This may happen without the above "fans" ever developing a relationship with the track's author. One listener or group on a P2P network is not a fan; not the way I would use that word. Fans want to know what's coming out next; they want to sit up front to see you perform; they want to be invited to a special release party.

So what role will fans play in the future? They will be your base customers, but not your big profits. If you have 5,000 guaranteed fans who will spend $3 for anything you distribute, that's $15,000 guaranteed gross that you can count on to finance a project. It may not be much, but it's better than 50,000 "friends" who will pay zero dollars if they can get the music for free. Long-tail theorists would argue otherwise. They would say that it's better to have 50,000 downloads, period. But "buyers" like that are fleeting. They will find something else to focus on tomorrow, and never pay you. Nope, 5,000 people who will pay a buck or two is far better in the long run than 50,000 people who pay nothing. From those paying 5,000 you can finance projects. Some will pay off, some will not, but you will always have a financial infrastructure. Labels and managers know this, and will look carefully at your sales records and fan base before they sign you.

But fans alone will not bring in the big bucks. For that you need placements. This will be covered in other parts of this book. See the questions on licensing, publishing, and 360 Deals.

So get fans. It's basically your only job as an artist. Which brings us to the next question.

What Social Networks Are Worth Joining to Get More Fans and Sell More Music?

Simple answer: As many as you have time for.

Want some priorities?

→ Facebook
→ MySpace
→ Twitter

This trifecta is mandatory for any career at this point, but each one works a bit differently. Always remember theses rules when marketing:

Step 1. Turn strangers into friends.
Step 2. Turn friends into customers.
Step 3. Turn customers into vendors.

Facebook is great for the first one. But, since Facebook doesn't allow you an infinite number of "friends," you'll need a way to aggregate their direct e-mail addys so you can service them outside of the FB environment. In other words, you'll have to start deleting friends from your account to make room for new friends as you reach the 5,000 mark.

That will be quite awkward, but if you've been prepping your friends from day one to communicate with you directly through e-mail, not impossible. Or you might be thinking, "5,000 friends/fans—that's so far down the road I don't need to think about it." But you do. It will happen faster than you think if you've got something special.

MySpace is not as hip as it used to be, but it's still a great tent-pole site, and it allows you to have over 20,000 "friends." It gives you a solid footprint in the proverbial sand of the beach called the Internet, and it's free. If you're just starting out, MySpace can be used in lieu of a website, but this should only be temporary. Not having your own website or app (or both) is just unprofessional.

And lastly, there is Twitter. Twitter is a way to play the Pied Piper with your fans: tell them where you are, provide breaking news, direct them to your website for a special release or performance. However, many people think that this is the end-all of their marketing, and that is a serious mistake. This is only Step 1. All social networks are merely Step 1. You still need to make people customers, and that means harvesting them to your own mailing list and serving them on a personal level. More on that in the next section on mailing lists.

Here are some other sites worth investigating:

- → YouTube (a must-have)
- → TubeMogul
- → Metacafe
- → Revver
- → Dailymotion
- → Buzz (Google)
- → Blip
- → Sclipo
- → Howcast
- → 5min
- → Graspr
- → Yahoo
- → AOL
- → Imeem
- → Jango

Don't waste your time trying to be famous on all of these. And don't become a social networking junkie. It's important to make new fans, not become a weirdo who tells people when they woke up, what ice cream they are buying, etc.

How Can I Maintain an Efficient Mailing List That Works?

Now, I'm not a professional e-mail marketer, so why am I answering this question? Well, many of my readers who've been on my list know that I run a tight ship. Since 1999 I have successfully managed one of the biggest opt-in lists in the music space, over 14,000 addys, all of which are "clean." Not an easy task. Many people claim to have lists that are bigger, but I can tell you, and you'll see why by the end of this answer, that most of them are either fooling you or fooling themselves. If you're turning to this question, then you are way ahead of the marketing curve than most of your peers, and probably further along in your career than you realize.

Too many artists, managers, producers, whoever, focus on Facebook or Twitter as the mainstay of communication with their customer/fan base, and have allowed the old-fashioned e-mail list to fall by the wayside. This is a big mistake, but it's an easy one to make. ISPs and spam laws have made it very confusing regarding what you can and cannot do in this area. Many people get tired of 550 and 501 returns (and I'm not talking about Levi's) and see that the response to their bulk e-mail is minimal. Meanwhile Facebook and Twitter provide instant responses. So it feels more effective. But I think you'll see that if you add up the actual dollars you've earned, more come from the people you're corresponding with directly than those you're tweeting. Why? Because we tend to need a personal connection before we part with our money.

So what are the issues with e-mail lists?

→Spam Laws
→Returns
→Maintenance

Spam Laws

People who don't like to receive promotional e-mails or who don't like what you're saying in your e-mail will often call you a spammer and threaten to report you to . . . someone. Don't listen. If they opted in via a form on your website, and you offer a means for them to opt out at any time, that already disqualifies you as spam under the so-called spam in a can law. (Even if you're selling junk, if you do all the above it's still hard for them to really complain to anybody.) They can ask to be removed from your list, and if they do you should do it ASAP. You're trying to make friends, not enemies.

Returns

550, 503, and 501 errors are common with any list containing over 700 names. The reason for most of these errors is that the person has abandoned the address but didn't tell you. They moved over to Gmail or something else that was free, like many during the mass migration of 2005, when AOL and others gave up trying to charge for e-mail accounts. In the sidebar "What Causes Returns?" is a list of common reasons for these errors and how to stop them.

Spam

Aside from a dead addy another reason for a return is that your e-mail was pegged as spam. Even though you may be sending an e-mail to someone who wants to receive it and has a valid addy, it can still get into their spam folder, because ISPs have filters that try to decrease spam based on common factors such as:

➜Too many capitalized words
➜Hyperlinks
➜Long subject matter banners
➜Content over 700 words

In other words, all the things that promotional materials use.
If you want to minimize the chance of being dumped into a spam folder, send out *text only* messages and throttle your

sending program to only send a few at a time. How many e-mails are sent each second depends on the size of your list, but between 7 and 15 e-mails every five seconds is a safe amount. AOL, for example, will roadblock all emails from your addy if you fire too many AOL addys at them at once. Only the first dozen or so will get through, and the others will get returned or quarantined into spam folders. This is also true of MSN, EarthLink, and many older services.

You'll notice that sometimes in a bulk sending a specific person will successfully receive an e-mail from you that contains several "spam elements," and then in the next sending it gets rejected and sent back. What up with that? Don't AOL and Gmail have consistent filters? No. This secret is covered in the very next section.

Maintenance and Bad Address Filters

I'm going to tell you a secret about ISPs and e-mail that few people know. When you send an e-mail to a friend, it doesn't always travel the same route. Even if the person is in the next room, that e-mail might get routed through a server 1,000 miles away before it hits your roommate. You probably knew this, but here's what you may not know. Each server in the chain of servers that pass the e-mail around has its own set of spam filters, which all work a little differently, but here's the best part—the routing is dynamic. This means that the series of spam filters/servers that your e-mail encounters on one route to your roommate will be different each time you send something to them. This makes it impossible to keep up with each route's filters. ISPs do this to help eliminate spam, by fooling bulk senders who typically shotgun thousands of e-mails at once, but it also means that legitimate e-mail lists are hurt.

One of the main trips for spam filters is how many returns or 550 errors the sender's address is generating. Yes, ISPs can see that info, but the screwed-up thing is that you could be getting 550 errors because of *inconsistent filtering*, and this will cause a return, which causes more 550 errors, which causes more returns. And on and on. How can you stop this madness? How can you figure out which addresses are truly dead and which ones are just fickle and jamming your rep with the ISP?

There are programs that will "ping" every addy on your list to see if it's still operating, but there are good reasons not to trust many of them. By pinging every name on your list they are doing exactly what ISPs flag as spam. So that is like trying to scare away a shark by splashing around in the water. What you want is a program that attaches to your actual mass e-mail sender that will keep a log as you send out e-mails. This log would assign a code to any returned e-mail depending on why it's returned—or not returned. Yes, you will need a code for "successfully delivered" as well, because sometimes you'll get a return on a particular addy and sometimes not, simply because of the route it took. After several failed attempts to reach the recipient, the program would intelligently conclude that this is truly a dead addy and delete the addy automatically from your list. This will streamline your list without alerting the ISPs to what you're doing.

It will take a few sendings, but if you're sending out flyers once a month it should not take more than three months to pare down the addy, making it a "clean" list: one where almost every name is deliverable. *Having a slim list is VERY important. When ISPs see mail going through with few returns, they assume that you're OK.*

What Causes Returns

Below are a few things that can lead to various types of 501 and 550 returns:

1. Invalid domain names. If you want to double-check, just try accessing the domain (website), and if it's not found, that's your confirmation that the e-mail address is defunct.

2. Mailbox full. The e-mail address is still valid, but the user is on vacation and their mailbox filled up because they're not clearing it out every day.

3. Invalid recipient/unknown user. Might as well delete. Some spam filters will actually reject suspected spam e-mails with this error, so there's a chance that the e-mail address is valid, but your e-mails aren't going to get through regardless. The person at the other end probably has to add you to a "white list" in order to get your e-mails.

4. Server timed out. If you see these e-mails bouncing again, delete them, although some of them may be OK addresses that are having temporary server problems. However, usually the e-mails hang around and try to get delivered over the course of a few days, so if they still can't be delivered after several attempts over several days, those addresses are suspect.

5. Request confirmation. Sometimes a server will request confirmation. This is an annoying feature of some spam filters; if they don't know you, they'll send you an e-mail that you have to respond to, and then they'll deliver your original e-mail.

Here are a few tips for "cleaning" your e-mail list to lubricate the bulk-sending process.

1. Filter out *all* AOL names, as well as MSN, EarthLink, and Gmail and put them each in a separate list.

2. Segregate names into the following format:name1@name.com,name2@name.com,name3@name.com.

3. After you've done all that, import the list into Word or a similar word processor and:

4. Run a "sort" function to alphabetize.

5. Eliminate any duplicates.

6. You should now have a main list with all names alphabetized except the AOL, MSN, Gmail, etc. names that are in separate lists.

7. Reinsert the AOL names, scattering them every 50 names or so.

8. Do the same with MSN, EarthLink, etc. Scatter the domains so that a single domain is not being bombarded at once.

9. Set a throttle so that not all addresses are being serviced at once. It will take hours to service a list over 5,000, but you'll know that most of them are getting through.

Having read all this, disbelieve ANYONE who tells you that they have a list of 50,000 to 100,000 or more names, unless they have someone working for them full-time just on this. It's simply highly improbable for one person with today's technology to maintain a "clean" list that large, with only 24 hours in a day.

How Do You Make Money from Music Other than Selling CDs?

Believe it or not, despite a 30 percent decrease in CD sales in the US since 2005, CDs continue to be the number-one income producer for music labels. Will this last another 10 years? Hard to say. But it's hard to beat the profit margin for something that costs about $1 to manufacture but that you can sell for between $10 and $16. But we'll have to try.

Here are the other revenue streams for music that even a beginner can get with.

Licensing for Film and TV

Every time you hear music in a movie or on TV (called a "synchronization"), two groups of people are being paid from the "sync rights": 1) the party that owns the composition (song), which includes all the writers and publishers; and 2) the party that owns the master recording, which includes the record label and the artist.

If you're just starting out, then chances are that you are all the above. This means that you can afford to compete with established names. Think about it: If a TV license goes for $5,000 (not untypical), and the money has to be split between the writer, publisher, artist, and label, then everyone makes about $1,250. This split is usually what drives up sync licensing fees. In major motion pictures these fees can get as high as $1,000,000 for the use of just 30 seconds of a popular song in the opening credits. But . . . if you're all the parties rolled into one, you can afford to compete. Make no mistake; even though almost every director making a Hollywood blockbuster wants an established hit for their opening credits, they will often have to settle for something more affordable and lesser known.

Being easy to deal with goes a long way with music supervisors (who pipeline music to films and TV producers) when they have 15 songs to negotiate for a soundtrack. Be flexible, but try to avoid giving into "all-in rights" deals.

These are deals where the performance monies that you should get from ASCAP, BMI, or SESAC, which you earn when the movie plays on TV, go to the producer instead of the composer. Producers always ask for them. You're expected to put up a fight. Don't disappoint.

Greeting Cards

Hallmark spends millions a year paying royalties for musical cards. Every time a card is sold, the writer and artist get about nine cents each. Some cards that sell for $3.50 pay royalties in the hundreds of thousands. Don't turn your nose up at these sales. They add up to big bucks.

Ringtones

This is obvious. For some reason the same public that screams that CDs are too expensive (at roughly 60 cents a song) will gladly pay $2.99 for a 20-second clip of music to be used in their phone. Ringtones make up about $2 billion a year in revenues for the music business.

In the not-too-distant past, in order to sell your music as a ringtone, you had to make a deal with an aggregator and give up a large percentage of your royalties. That's because most phones would only accept ringtones from sites that had a dedicated codec for the phone. But now, publishing your own ringtones has never been easier. All you need is a page on a social network (free) to sell them from. These days most savvy people have the software to convert just about any sound file into a ringtone for almost any phone. The future suggests that accessibility will be moving in favor of the consumer. Meaning that you can sell your own music as a ringtone to anybody, without a middleman.

Do it.

Commercials

Ads are considered to be the crown jewel of sync licenses. When Nike used the Beatles' "Revolution," it reportedly paid over

$500,000 for a six-month license. Amazing. Commercials are high-stakes poker for music. Agencies will pay more than top dollar for music for which a greeting card company will pay nothing up front, expecting you to get paid off the back-end sales.

Why can ad agencies pay more? Because they are not paying. Their client is—the sneaker company, the car company, etc. They've already spent millions on the ad campaign.

Now, to get these gigs is not easy. You'll probably need an agent and a lot of connections. It can take years to get a single placement. But it's worth it.

Games

Ever see a video game without music? No. Once upon a time video game companies paid a lot for the clips and loops used in games like *Grand Theft Auto*. Now, game companies have gotten savvy, and operate with the same degree of chumming as record labels. But they are buying music, and that makes them our new best friend.

License fees range from $0 with $2 on the back end per sale to $25,000 buyouts.

Websites

Every time a website loads into your computer and music plays, that website pays a fee to a company called SoundExchange. You can register with them for free and get paid when your music plays on many different sites. Give your music away for the first month if you have to. These streams add up. And speaking of streams . . .

Streaming Royalties

Every subscription service pays, as do all the ad-revenue-based services like Spotify. Getting your music on these servers may not mean that you can buy a house with the tiny royalties split, but it could mean a car payment or two.

What Do Major Labels Really Want from a New Artist in Order to Sign Them?

If you've turned to this chapter or made it this far in a straight read-through of this book, then you are probably serious about your career. You will read a lot of blogs and "chats" about how the major labels are dead and no one really needs a record deal anymore. This is not really true if you want to sell millions of records. It may become true someday in some abstract future, but for now there has never been an artist that has sold millions of records without the help of a major label. (Although plenty of artists make a good living without one.)

If you're looking at a label, then you have to ask the logical question of why would a label want you? Investing in an artist can get expensive. Labels often invest up to a million dollars for each artist they sign. Most of the artists they sign never make back that investment for the label. Labels claim that only one in 10 make back their investment. I think it's probably more like 1 in 6. But no matter. It's risky to throw a million bucks at four or five jamming kids and hope to turn that into a moneymaking venture.

So the qualities labels look for are ones that will reduce their risk:

➔ Lots of fans
➔ Lots of show dates where those fans show up and pay
➔ Lots of hits on your website
➔ Lots of record sales

What is "lots"? Each label is different, but here's a basic guideline.

➔ If you have over 5,000 *legitimate* "friends" on any well-known social network (Facebook, MySpace, etc.), that is good.

➔If you are playing out three to six times a month in venues that hold at least several hundred people, that is good. They do not have to be big arenas. Small clubs qualify.

➔If your website is constantly being hit, with about 1,000 new visitors a month, that is good.

➔If through your own efforts you can show that you've sold either 10,000 CDs or about 10,000 singles downloads, that is good.

The above is a basic building block. After this will come other things that are not as easy to quantify: your musical ability, looks, and most important, your attitude. No one likes to invest in someone who shows contempt for them. In the movies, artists love to diss their labels. In real life they don't get signed if they do. And if they are signed they often get dropped.

Attitude is the number-one ingredient. Major labels tend to believe that if an artist is a great musician but has a bad attitude, they should pass. That's because it is easier to give a mediocre musician a few music lessons than change someone's personality. That doesn't mean they want to sign a wimp who is a "company man" or kiss-ass. But they also don't want to feel that someone they have given money to is going to treat them with disrespect.

Being signed to a label means that you're part of a company stable. You work with your fellow artists who are also on that label, helping them as they help you. It means that the label is your partner in crime. You don't get to make all the creative decisions on your own. For many people this sucks. If you feel that way, then don't pursue a major label deal, but also don't expect to ever sell enough records on your own to be able to buy a big house and drive a fancy car. The odds are extremely small.

Am I Too Old for a Record Deal?

No! Many artists were not signed till they were in their late 20s. (Counting Crows, for example.) The names are too countless to list here, but they number in the thousands.

It's true that in the past five years we've seen younger signings in the female department, but we've also seen some people breaking age records in the other direction in the male department.. And while it's true that this industry worships youth, these things also work in cycles. In 2009 a major label deal was given to a 45-year-old. It was his first deal and came with a $500,000 advance. I believe that we will begin to see "older" recording artists in the next few years. The pendulum is swinging back toward mature artists with things to say, not just bubblegum.

There is also the fact that many people lie about their age. Many top stars have been lying for so long that we accept their lies as fact. They do this because they know how their age plays a role in public perception.

Your age is your business. Keep it that way. If you do not look your age, then you should definitely not worry about it. Don't make age an issue and it will not be one.

What Music Biz Blogs Are Worth My Time?

There seem to be literally hundreds of them, and not nearly enough time to read them all. Which ones are best? The Internet age has given anyone with a laptop a voice. Never in the history of publishing has there been a more democratic process than the blog. What makes a blog "good"? Well, if it's popular, I guess. What makes it popular? If people like reading what's on it.

Never, however, confuse popularity with *truthiness*. Many people like reading all kinds of things just for amusement, not because they reflect a global reality. Case in point are the many blogs that seem to be about the music business but in fact are anti-music-business blogs designed to trash the music space and major labels. Many people subscribe to these blogs, and so they are considered "good" by the standard I outlined above, but that does not mean that they are telling the *whole truth* and nothing but. Quite the reverse. Once a blog finds an audience, it tends to cater to it.

As an extreme example, let's say I had a blog about cats that attracted about 10 new subscribers a month, and then I wrote an article one day that said I hated dogs and suddenly I got 1,000 new subscribers. I might be interested in writing more anti-dog articles—especially if I planned on selling advertising on my blog. More eyeballs means more money. But even if I have no advertising, I might like the idea that I now have 1,000 new readers, and I might start to write more anti-dog articles. I might even convince myself that being anti dog is the same as being pro cat, so I'm not selling out. But I am. They are not the same.

In the music space we have blogs that are pro ISPs and pro P2P/BitTorrenting. These are, by default, anti-music-business, even though they do not see themselves that way, because they encourage people to think that "information should be free," and therefore they are anti-copyright. These people probably go to sleep each night thinking that they are doing the music business a lot of good by encouraging people to steal music. Somehow.

So therefore I've taken the time to tell you what the bias is for each of the following blogs. The fact that I disagree with the agenda of some of these blogs does not stop me from subscribing to them. Why subscribe to a blog that I disagree with? Because I want to hear what it is saying (and sometimes I see a blog agreeing with me, even though it won't admit it).

I am also quite curious about how some of these blogs might begin to change their viewpoints in the future, as public opinion starts to shift back toward honoring copyrights. Will they track with the zeitgeist to keep an audience, or dissolve into oblivion?

Music Think Tank
www.musicthinktank.com

This blog features interesting articles by entry-level people in the biz. It has a decidedly young perspective, but that does not mean that it's an invalid or inferior one. Just that its bias is toward "innovative" (and sometimes untested) theories.

Most of the writing is very good, and I have read many pieces that I agree with. Something to watch out for is that these writers tend to promote their friends as valid services. There's nothing wrong with that if you let your audience know what you are doing. But they don't, so I'm telling you here. If you see one author endorsing the services of another, there is probably a great deal of camaraderie in play rather than a track record of actual service. But not always.

HypeBot
www.hypebot.com

Although this blog leans toward having a tech bias, this is the most neutral of the blogs I have found. It positions itself as forward thinking instead of getting mired in the politics of who is right about P2P. Occasionally it takes sides, and when it does it's usually with the ISPs.

Lefsetz Letter
www.lefsetz.com

Angry rantings by very established blogger Bob Lefsetz that you must read simply because he's a force who posts three times a day. Like an auto accident, you cannot help but rubberneck just to find out what he is ranting about now. Invariably he's pandering to his audience made up of mostly disgruntled, male, white, over 50 ex-record execs who are lamenting being obsolete and ultimately booted from their cushy, overpaid gigs at major labels. So naturally they love it every time Bob says the sky is falling and the record biz is dying.

His other audience is young bands who think his "screw the

labels" attitude is cool. God help them. When people in the know who are successful in the biz respond to his posts, they usually disagree with him. Regardless, he's probably the best opinionist in the music blogosphere.

So if I disagree with him, why am I recommending that you subscribe? Well, he's a talented writer, who occasionally makes a good point (although he'll likely contradict himself in his next blog entry), and he is read by a great many people, so it helps to be informed as to what he "believes."

Rock & Rap Confidential
www.rockrap.com

Veteran journalist Dave Marsh always has a very pro-artist (often super-liberal) take on stories of disenfranchisement in the music space. Sometimes he posts other people's work. Good stuff. Dave is a straight shooter.

Dean's List
home.earthlink.net/~deankay/
DeanKay_TheDean'sList.html

Dean Kay is on the board of ASCAP, and puts together his letter by paraphrasing other people's articles. Nicely done. Two thumbs up. His bias is clearly very pro-copyright and anti-tech. Although for reasons that defy me he does seem to give a lot of clicks to the pro-tech site below.

Digital Music News
www.digitalmusicnews.com

The intellectual puppet for the technology industry disguising itself as neutral journalism. It's not even close to the journalistic standard for neutral. This is, to put it bluntly, the Fox News of the ISP/label wars. It always sides with the ISPs. Why a pro-artist company like Harry Fox advertises on it is beyond me. However, its viewpoints, while unabashedly one-sided, are very articulate, well researched, and worth attending to. Subscribe.

Moses Supposes
www.mosesavalon.com/mosesblog

My blog. I don't post as often or as consistently as some of my contemporaries above. But you'll usually find facts here that others ignore because they would destroy their arguments. I've broken stories that *Billboard* won't print for fear of offending advertisers. I have no advertisers. I have a very pro-artist, *copyrightist* bias and believe that ISPs are literally at war with the creative industries. Their goal is to devalue catalogs and then buy them someday for pennies on the dollar.

M.E.L.O.N. Feed: Multimedia and Entertainment Law Online News
www.beatblog.typepad.com

Legal abstracts that are worth knowing about. Every month decisions are made in courts around the country that affect the world of music. M.E.L.O.N. makes it easy to understand and digest them.

Music Technology Policy
www.musictechpolicy.com

Contributed to mostly by Chris Castle, who leans more toward the creative side than the technology side. Chris is funny and on point. Subscribe.

Conclusion

So now you know how to avoid a few land mines, but you also know enough to get you into some real trouble. So to speak. A little bit of knowledge is often a dangerous thing, as the old saying goes. That's why there are four other parts to this book.

The next section will take you through the most important first threshold in your career—your first deal. Which is often a really bad one. Why? Well, you're often eager and still ignorant; a bad combination for success and a great prerequisite for all the song sharks and swindlers. But don't worry; everyone has a "lousy first deal" story. Hopefully with the answers provided you'll be able to contribute one less.

Turn the page.

PART 2

I Just Made My First Lousy Little Deal

Questions and Answers for Those Who Have Gotten Serious

Introduction

So you're no longer quibbling over who is the songwriter or the producer, or who plays what in the band, or that just because your friend owns the garage you rehearse in, that doesn't make him the producer or the manager. Congratulations, you've survived Stage 1 of your music career: you know what you're responsible for and what you need to get someone else to do for you. You know enough to know that there is a lot more to know. You're teetering on the cusp of the difference between total amateur and semi-pro.

In chapter 2 you'll see the answers to many of the questions facing those of you who have just crawled out from inside the garage. It can be a scary transition, but know that you're not alone and that every top pro was at this same stage once. You'll get through it, with a little help from your friends.

Why Are All These Music Managers So Afraid/Lazy About Signing New Artists?

An easy question to answer. Managers are not artists. They are business people. Each client they take on involves a great deal of risk. Let's break this down a bit.

There are two types of managers: the local dude who books local acts, and the established manager who has national acts and their headaches to deal with. I'm presuming this question goes more toward type two. If you're having trouble getting type one to "manage" you, then, to quote Shakespeare, "The fault lies not within our stars, but in ourselves."

So the national manager is what you want, and what you're whining about in the question. "Why doesn't Irving Azoff, Simon Renshaw, or David Sonenberg sign me and make me a star? I've got great material; a huge fan base of about 20,000 'friends' on MySpace; several songs licensed to major motion pictures; I play 30 colleges a year, each paying me $7,000 a show; and I'm No. 15 on the iTunes download chart for this month, with over 8,000 downloads of my cool single. Why can't I get a top-flight manager?"

Okay, here goes:

Managers need to evaluate every new act the way a bank evaluates a loan application. What does a bank look at? Income, debt, holdings, and . . . stability. That's a big factor in determining if you get a bank loan. Your income may be so-so, but if the bank thinks your potential is super due to rock-solid, incremental growth, you may get a loan that slightly exceeds your debt ratio (a fancy bank term that simply means the relationship between how much you owe and how much you make, as an indicator of how easily you can make your loan payments)..

Conversely, many a wealthy person has been turned down for a loan because the conditions under which they acquired their wealth may not be stable factors within the market in which they acquired it, or within the person themselves; for example, if they are rich due to a talent that has a time limit, like a sports figure in the seventh year of his contract. Sure, he has made $3 million a year for the past six years, but what will he make in the next five years? That's the key question. Another example would be a person who wants a construction loan to renovate his five-apartment complex. He's got lots of real estate holdings, but they make poor collateral in a down market.

Many bands have good income today, but where will they be in five years? What is their professional equity? To people who manage a Golden Goose heritage act, like the Eagles, they might not consider hype built mostly on social networks to be enough collateral to allocate about $100,000 worth of resources, just to get started. Yes, a big manager makes a large investment in any new act they take on:

> ➔ Press releases and PR to announce the signing and let everyone know who the new manager is, if they want to deal with the act: $7,000
> ➔ Lawyers' fees for negotiating the contract: $4,000
> ➔ Parsing of staff time to handle various issues, troubleshoot, goalie, and do various other menial tasks that if not done will mess everything up: $2,000/month or $24,000/year
> ➔ PR for several months during new releases, signings, etc.: $3,000/month for about six months (sporadically), or $18,000

We're already over $100K, and we haven't even gotten to your share of the office electricity, faxes, messengers, and the pimply kid who picks you up at the airport.

When it's an act that is already bringing in $30,000,000 a year, $100,000 is not an issue. But if you're barely bringing in even $200,000 a year, a $100,000 outlay isn't looking so good. Even if as the manager you take an average cut of 20%, it will take you two-and-a-half years to break even. That's assuming that the act continues to make $200,000 a year. Many seek management at this level as they are peaking. But now that you're dealing with a top-flight dude, your marketing and promotion expenses will go up, up, up. So your act will need to make more just to cover the new overhead (see the questions on tour and recording budgets, pages 113 and 116).

Conversely, a manager can easily afford to lure an international act away from an old management contract, giving up 20% by offering to do the same job for 5%. Five percent of $30,000,000 is $1,500,000. Shredding even half a million to snatch such an act is well worth the investment.

"But what about the deals where a big shot signs a new act that hasn't even had their first album?" Almost without exception these are acts that are signed to major labels, and there is a close relationship between the manager and the head of the label. Even though there are almost no statistics to use to scale the artist's income, there are advances and the promises of some sales and publishing. So, in many cases the manager is taking very little risk, because he knows that his longtime buddy at the label will not let him hang in the wind. He knows how many first pressings there will be, and what the advance schedule is. So he knows that at least he will get some sort of decent commission for his efforts.. He may also be signing this act as a strategy because he has another client on that same label, and this gives him more leverage.

So, before calling a big shot, do the math. The magic number is 7. It should not cost the manager more than 1/7th of your annual income to get started. This way he recoups in less than 15 months.

What's a Good Deal, Anyway?

A fair question, without a fair answer. What a good deal is depends on what your goals are for your career and how desperately you are in need of what is being offered. Interestingly enough, one of my readers, Jason (Dyer) Roth, who wrote in with this question then proceeded to answer it himself with the impressive chart he made below—reprinted here with his permission. (I tweaked it a bit.)

	The Good (For the artist)	The Bad (For both, which is also the good for both as it's balanced.)	The Ugly (For the artist)
ADVANCE/ALBUM COMMITMENT & ROYALTIES	$300,000 Advance (each album) with a two-album commitment. Artist and label split all receipts 50/50 after recoupment.	$50,000 Advance, per album with no commitment for any future recordings. Artist gets 12%–15% AFTER recoupment.	$50,000 Advance for eight albums that must be delivered by the artist on his or her own dime. **Artist gets 12%-15% AFTER recoupment.**
MERCHANDISING	90/10 split in artist's favor with a $100,000 advance.	75/25 split in artist's favor with a $35,000 advance.	No merchandising share. Label gets it all with $0 advance.
PUBLISHING	Artist gets to keep 100% of all rights to songs.	75/25 split in artist's favor for all revenue produced by licensing. No monies from publishing are used to recoup other debts.	Label gets all publishing rights, and uses monies to pay off debts from other aspects of the deal.
CONCERTS	Once $100,000 tour support from label is recouped, 20% of receipts go to label on a per album basis. No tour receipts are used to pay back other advances from label.	Once $100,000 tour support from label is recouped, 50% from receipts goes to label. 25% goes toward other debt.	No tour support and all receipts go to pay back debts from other parts of the deal.
NOTES TO THINK ABOUT	Overall, in a good contract the label realizes the band is worth their time/money. Merchandising and concert receipts are shared in a healthy/respectful way.	This is a basis for most new contracts. The label provides some upfront money; however, if the band does not perform well, no matter how hard they work they will not receive another penny until the label decides that the upfront investment has been satisfied…this could take years. Don't spend your money in this case, or you may be a (literally) starving artist.	You will only get $50,000 to be a slave for 13 years and will probably not be able to fulfill the concert as a starving artist.

What Is a 360 Deal? How Is It Different from an "Old School" Deal, and Do I Need to Sign Either to Be Successful?

New so-called 360 Deals on major labels want a piece of everything the artist makes. They get their name because a circle has 360 degrees, and these deals collect revenue from all directions: sales, touring, licensing, publishing, acting, modeling, merchandise— you name it. They also go by the name "all-in" deals. (Not to be confused with "all-in" budgets or "all-in" royalties.)

They offer big bucks, higher percentages, and look and feel like the major label deals of yesteryear, with the big press releases, and the label executives shaking your hand in offices perched high above some big-city skyline. But are they like the old deals? Could it be that these deals are merely a façade, and the label may be committing fraud even *before* the toner on the contract is dry?

Typically splits and advances on major label 360 Deals look like this:

➔ Record sales and master licensing: 50/50, with an advance of about $250,000

➔ Publishing: 50/50, with a special advance of about $50,000

➔ Touring: 85/15 in favor of the artist, with an advance of about $50,000

➔ Merchandise: 85/15 in favor of the artist, with an advance of about $25,000

➔ Personal appearances/endorsements: 85/15 in favor of the artist

➔ Website/fan club: 50/50, with an advance of about $25,000

➔ Acting: 90/10 in favor of the artist

Sounds good. Old-style deals only paid about a 9% royalty on record sales; this one pays 50%. And advances total $400,000. Where do I sign? But there's a catch to each of the points above.

First of all, the touring, merchandise, and fan club advances will certainly be gobbled up fast by the cost of launching each of these ventures. The publishing advance you'll get to keep most of, thankfully. About 80% of the recording advance will be eaten up by the album production costs. And then we get to the splits.

Is 50% Really More than 9%?

If 9% in the old deals gave you about a $1 royalty, then 50% would surely give you about $5, right? Sure. If you got 50% of the *gross*. But let's do the funky record company math. These deals pay everything on the *net*. And the net is hard to figure out, since the labels tend to hide many of their deductions until you get a royalty statement. Typically there are a series of deductions.

Even though singles and downloads will someday overtake CD sales, we're going to use CD sales as our example. CD sales still make up over 75% of a signed artist's recorded music revenue, and probably will for years to come (see page 64 for more on why this is so). So, let's take the gross amount earned from a CD sale, about $12, and deduct 20% as a distribution fee, leaving $9.60. Then the label will subtract all recording, duplication, and other expenses. The big loophole is that they define "recording expenses" as all costs related to production and distribution. This includes the mechanical royalties[1] they pay to the songwriters. If the songwriter is the same as the artist, then they are merely giving money to the artist with one hand and taking it back with the other.

---

1. Mechanical royalties: The money record companies pay songwriter/publishers (who are the same as the artist about 50% of the time) for the right to reproduce the songs in a recording. The fee is set by law at 9.1 cents per song.

Since the songwriter's royalties are generally about 90 cents a record, and duplication expenses are about $1 a CD, this brings the net down to about $7. (If you look in the chapter "The Major Label Deal from the Point of View of the Record Company," in my first book, *Confessions of a Record Producer*, you can see a complete and detailed list—the only one in print, I might add—of how the label's costs take a $12 gross to about $5 net.) Suffice it to say that even though the label has increased your royalty on record sales more than 500% from where it was, the monetary difference is only about 70 cents. Or roughly up to $2 a unit.

That's still better than $1 a unit, but is it worth giving up 5%–20% slices of your merchandise, touring, and even acting revenue? The answer depends on what you're using the record deal for. If you're, say, an actor, with a budding film/TV career, who writes his own songs, and you're using the album to bolster your profile—this deal will eat you alive. If you just want record sales, and you're not much of a writer, then a 360 Deal is great for you.

Now, if you're saying, "I may be only a recording artist, but I write my own songs—all of them, so I should pass on a 360 offer, right?" No. Two reasons why:

1. You'll still need a publishing deal to get a big advance for your songs, so why not incentivize your label? Make them work harder to earn more. Since everything is based on a percentage, more for them means more for you.

2. What makes you think that by Album three the label is still going to use all your material? They don't have to use any of your material, y'know. Think you can beat the odds? Chew on this—over 90% of *all* artists start using what are called "non-controlled"[2] songs by the third album. We can't all be Bob Dylan or Van Morrison.

---

2. A "controlled composition" is industry jargon for a song where the artist owns all the rights. A "non-controlled" song is one where the artist either co-wrote the song with someone outside the group, or is recording a cover tune, remake, or a new song that has never been published and that he or she did not write.

Another reason is that you might have no choice. Many publishers who are affiliated with major labels (like Warner Records and Warner-Chappell Publishing) are now requiring lateral integration as part of their offer. In other words, if you want the record deal with XYZ Records, you have to go with XYZ Publishing as well.

But What About the Question?

Okay, okay, so I drifted a bit off the topic. I wanted to clearly define the difference between these two types of deals. So, to be successful do you have to sign either an old-school deal, where you only get 9%–12% of the record sales but get to keep everything else, or a newer 360 Deal, where you get 40% of the record sales but you have to share everything you make with the label?

The short answer is—YES!!

Your deal may not be with a record label per se—it may be a manager's deal, or a production deal—but sooner or later, if you're at the stage of your career where you've proven yourself to be a worthy candidate for stardom, and the next move is the infusion of a shitload of cash to make it all happen, then yes— someone, somewhere is going to want a piece of you. What form that piece will take is the real question, and the real answer is just as simple: *It depends on how much money is on the table.* Here's a barometer: If the advances from the label total more than four times what you're making with music on your own, then you're crazy in this economy to turn down the deal without a solid alternative. If your total sales from CDs, downloads, licensing, and touring equal a gross of $50,000 over the four years you've been busting your hump, and now, with this offer, you'll clear $400,000 from the combined advances *alone*, and acquire a well-experienced partner to boot—take it!

If, however, you're grossing $100,000 a year from all the above, plus another $100,000 from the day job that you'll be giving up, and the combined advances only equal three times that or $300,000, then negotiate for recorded music rights only, or just a P&D (Pressing and Distribution) Deal.

STOP!!! Now, this is just a meatball guideline. Don't worship it. Don't say, "Moses said I should turn down $500,000 because I'm already making five figures a year bagging groceries." You have to weigh a lot of factors. That's where lawyers, managers, and consultants earn their fees. So don't try this at home, kids. Consult an expert first!

Does a 360 Deal Guarantee a Greater Commitment to the Artist?

Didn't I just answer this question? Hmmm . . . no, not really. They are two separate questions when you break it down.

The truth is that 360 Deals are so new as of this writing in late 2010 that it's way too early to definitively answer a question like this. But we can use a bit of logic to make some reasonable guesses. Labels are greedy: like most businesses, and they want to make as much cash as possible off their investments. So I'm going to teach you a very basic lesson in business by getting you to think like a record label.

Let's say I have two identical music products by two different artists, but I invested $1,000 in artist "A" and $1,300 in artist "B." "A" delivered a critically acclaimed album that costs me $1 per unit to promote and yields a $4 profit for each sale. "B" made a record that sounds like everyone else. It costs me $1 per unit to promote but it yields $4.60 a sale. Both sell about the same in the first year.

Both "A" and "B" come to me for more money in the second year to bump up their promotion and increase their sales. I only have enough money to give to one. Which artist gets it? If you think I gave the money to "A" because some critics like their record more, then you're not in the music business game. Naturally, I'm happier with "B." It costs me a bit more to invest in them, but the promotion cost is about the same as "A," and the profit yield more than makes up for it in fewer than 400 sales. In the long run, "B" is a better investment.

In case you haven't figured out where I'm going with this analogy, "A" is the old-style deal that only focuses on music sales. "B" is the 360 Deal, which yields money from several sources for each sale (publishing, merchandise, etc.). From the label's viewpoint they are getting more per sale, and therefore will be more incentivized to push higher-yielding product. It's really that simple.

If your record company is going to be your true partner, and you believe in their ability to get you to the top of the pile, "B" is the better way to go. Yet there are many land mines to look out for in a 360 Deal. These are outlined in exhaustive detail in my other book, *Secrets of Negotiating a Record Contract*. Get it, if you plan to go to the next level.

Why Are There So Many Scam Companies That Claim to Help Indie Artists with Their Careers, and How Can I Avoid Them?

This is an easy one—downsizing. Let's say you're a major label executive making $250,000 a year. You lose your job. You go to another major label (there are only about 35 of them), but they are downsizing as well. So now what? You know the music trade, you have a great resume, and need to support a $250,000 lifestyle. You become a consultant, or start an "indie" music-related business.

This is the basis of almost every new music-business entity in the past 15 years. Since 1999, when the labels began to tighten their belts, executives have been axed and needed new income. They can't exactly go to work in another field, because their skill set of hanging out backstage is not really a good specialty for banking or medical work. So they hang out their shingle in an area with which they have built up experience—music. Some of these businesses are legit, but most disappear within a few years because they are not run with any degree of passion (or compassion) for the indie artist.

And don't think that this phenomenon is limited to only those in high-paying jobs. There are myriad companies started by people who interned for a hip indie label until it went out of business, or they were fired. They want to be in the music business, but decent jobs are very hard to come by—at least ones that pay well. Many of these people are smart enough to figure out that if they are going to work for peanuts, they might as well work for themselves and build a brand or a niche where they can be the king fish. These people can not attract big-name clients, at least not at first, so they target their services to the emerging artist. Is this dangerous? If they are all icing and no cake, you bet.

This section is not about the actual scams themselves. I have an entirely separate book for that called *Confessions of a Record Producer: How to Survive the Scams and Shams of the Music Business*. Here I'm going to do a bit of profiling.

The three most-traveled areas of the music *scam*isphere:

➜ Public Relations/SEO (Search Engine Optimization)
➜ Independent Promotion
➜ Digital Rights Aggregation

Let's look at all three up close.

Public Relations/SEO

I apologize for singling out publicists—there are a lot of good ones—but indie PR seems to rank high in the low-hanging fruit of the music scam arena. Why? Because any field where results cannot be quantified scientifically will attract scammers. In PR there are so many nebulous factors within which a professional can camouflage their incompetence.

The pitches and methods of these people almost without exception buck the established methods of doing things. Instead of a print campaign or servicing media, they will often talk their clients into a viral campaign to drive traffic to the client's site. They will rarely have a plan to monetize the traffic beyond this result. "Then you sell them CDs and downloads," they say. Does this sound familiar? This is very nickel and dime, and will probably not even justify their fees, which are often in the low four figures a month.

How do they get away with it? Viral efforts are essential these days, but usually in concert with a traditional campaign, not in lieu of one. Naive newbie artists who don't know much about PR see bigger artists doing viral and Internet-based campaigns, and so they figure that this is good for them, too. But they are missing the big picture: for bigger artists who have lots of cash for PR, viral and Internet campaigns work over a long period of time, like a year or two, and are only one part of a larger campaign that involves TV, print, and magazine placements. If you've only got a few grand in your PR budget, doing only viral advertising will increase SEO, but only temporarily.

Why do PR scamsters do this? Why not just do a traditional campaign? Because print placement in major publications requires deep contacts. PR scamsters usually have not been in the business long enough to develop the type of clout where they can pick up the phone and get you an interview in *Rolling Stone*, so they tell you it's a waste of time. Traditional print placement is also easier to audit. Clients can see a review or an article about themselves, and so they know that their publicist has done their job. Viral is too nebulous to track without real SEO knowledge. And watching the hits on your site triple is not the end result of SEO, as the scammer may tell you. It's the quality of those hits that counts. In other words, what was the conversion rate? How many of those hits became someone who singed up for a newsletter, or bought a download. That's what counts as effective PR/SEO.

Big stars have been with their publicists for many years, but PR scamsters in general don't really want long-term clients, because they don't have the resources to do a progressive campaign. They want many short-term clients that can cough up a few grand here and there. Thus, they will often advertise about the great number of clients they have, instead of the one or two top long-term clients that they do not have.

Real PR firms charge about $10,000 a month for a six-month campaign. If your prospective publicist is telling you that he or she can beat their antiquated methods with a few mouse clicks for $1,000 a month, then ask yourself a simple question. What makes their PR firm so smart? What do they know that firms charging 10 times as much do not? Are they the only genius in the field?

Sometimes the established method needs a kick in the pants. Artists know this; in fact, they resonate with the sentiment, and so they gravitate toward anyone with a cool, screw-the-old-school approach. But the reality is that often this is oversimplified advice and will lead to poor success. One prominent PR person who shows up at many music conferences is fond of saying that an interview in a major magazine or a sponsored tour from Nokia can be a career killer. Yikes. What the hell are they talking about? They are talking about indie cred, not sales. But unless I got it wrong, most acts who are serious enough to want to pay thousands for PR won't want cred as much as they want sales. You cannot pay the rent with cred. And who says that sales won't led to cred, anyway? This person does. It's their shtick. What they can't deliver they condemn.

Why does PR attract the most scammers? You don't need a degree to do PR, and if you're marketing yourself to indie musicians, you can even spin this into a positive "Hey, I went to school and it was all BS. Yeah, I left my major label marketing assistant gig because they are dinosaurs who couldn't track with new ideas. They don't even know how to manage privacy patterns on a social network, or do an MMS blog with an RSS feed."

Spot the Scammer

Maybe. Maybe that's true. Or maybe these new-wave PR maestros are just tireless and efficient self-promoters, with no real PR acumen.

PR is the easiest entry-level position in the business and has the highest turnover of *any* job in the industry. More people are hired and fired from in-house PR positions than from legal, accounting, advertising, and A&R departments combined. When they get the boot, where do they go? Usually they go out on their own. Some are great at what they do. But most are awful. How can you tell the difference? I'm going to tell you right now.

I get pitched by PR and SEO people all the time for my business. They want over $1,000 a month. One guy that I can recall positions himself as a "guru," claiming 100,000 subscribers to his blog and a hit book that tells it like it is. So I bit and did some research on his "firm" as part of my vetting process. Turns out that his YouTube account, which has PR lessons designed around his book, lists only 1,500 subscribers, and most of the videos were viewed fewer than 400 times.

This is inconsistent with someone who has 100,000 blog subscribers. His book is ranked on Amazon.com in the 350,000 zone. That means he sells about 25 books a month—in a good month.

In reality, my guess is that he may have a list of 100,000 e-mail addys that he pings each week via his blog, but many of them may be dead (see the section of this book on social networking and list management, page 123, for more on this). When I Googled his name I got fewer than 4,000 links. What does that mean? Well, if you Google my name you'll get about 35,000 links, and I only blog about once a month and do almost zero PR. If you're blogging every day or two, and you've in the PR business for several years, and the best you've got is 4,000 links, then it is you who should be paying *me* to do SEO/PR for you, not the other way around.

Anyone who is pitching you PR services should be able to do it effectively for themselves. Always do an "advanced search" on Google the minute anyone contacts you for your business. If it's PR-related and they have fewer than 20,000 links after being in the business for over five years, I recommend a pass.

On the very rare occasions when I hire a PR or SEO person, I don't pay for their time, I pay for placement. In other words, I don't pay by the month. I say, "I'll pay you X if you can get me on that show, get my ranking up to X, get my article positioned here or there." That is quantifiable. If they don't do it, they don't get paid. Period. None of this "Well, we need to try combining this thing with that thing for three more months," or, "I serviced your account, but it was a really busy month, and all my contacts are in the Hamptons till September." If they are not a huge PR firm, but rather someone who is working out of their apartment or a small office, they should be able to work on a results basis, at least for the first trial month.

In the social networking section I'll give you my distilled knowledge of the top 10 viral-marketing "gurus." The rest requires hard work. I'm no PR expert, but then again, this is not brain surgery. It's about 10% knowledge and 90% effort.

Independent Promotion

Coming in a close second in the bottom-feeding department are independent promoters. These guys pitch you that they can get your songs inserted into rotation at radio stations. They charge a lot for something for which it is very hard to do quality control. There has already been a great deal written about this profession (see the payola section, page 123, for more), so I won't waste page space here, but basically they operate along the same lines as PR scamsters. Their results cannot be quantified, so they can hide their incompetence.

I track many of these companies, and have acted as a sort of Better Business Bureau for the indie community. In 10 years of tracking these independent promoter types, only one name has consistently shown up as trustworthy: Howard Rosen. Having said that, it should also be noted that past performance is no guarantee of future success. I don't monitor the inner workings of his organization, and so this mention should not be taken as an endorsement.

Digital Rights Aggregators

Finally, in third place, but moving back in line in recent years, are digital rights aggregators, sometimes called digital labels or digital distribution deals. I'm going to call them DRAs for simplicity here. This used to be my number-one area of fraud against indie artists. I'm proud to say I helped some of these companies in their progress toward nonexistence, as well as helped others reach a high level of success.

As the indie label system deteriorates, you will see a great many companies following this service path. So far, many indie labels have become DRAs, which is a fancy name for a record company that has no inventory. They aggregate the rights to sell your music on the Internet and then hopefully collect the money, like a publisher. Some are great; some really, really suck.

In 2004, it was early in the game and very easy and cheap to set up an account at the few digital stores around at the time. No one really understood what reasonable terms were, because everything was so new. Many DRAs asked for exclusive rights, long terms, and high fees. But this fraudulent area started to drop behind PR after 2008, when one of the biggest offenders in the area of bad contract terms was sold to a larger company with more established ties. Although the transition to the new ownership was a rough one, according to blogs by members, the company now operates more efficiently than it did under the previous administration.

Today, many of the smaller, scammy digital rights companies have found it too expensive to compete with the larger DRAs that are dominating the market. With a great deal of advocacy as well as help from concerned artists, I and others have been able to set some standards in the DRA space that have taken root and made it far safer to do business with these entities than before. I have a chart on my website that analyzes the top companies:

www.mosesavalon.com. Some will turn into vital and thriving businesses (like TuneCore); others will wither and rot. If you know of a DRA that you like (or dislike), send me an e-mail.

Are Music Conferences a Waste of Time? Does Anyone Get Great Deals from Them?

Well, maybe for many people the idea of spending thousands of dollars to schlep through airports into hotels and cabs for several days, only to end up with a handful of business cards from people they will never remember and a swag bag containing a bunch of CDs that they don't care about, is cool. Maybe they just like to party out of town. Or maybe it's worth every dollar and minute they can spare.

They say you have to kiss a lot of frogs to find a prince. If you think so, there are a bevy of music business functions that serve this philosophy—from medium-grade ones like CMJ to high-end ones like MIDEM, where people with far more dollars than sense fly to the south of France and stay in four-star hotels just to mingle with French lingerie models. (Wait, that's starting to sound kinda cool . . .)

Some of these conferences are very useful, but most have become showcases for already financed acts, not places where true "emerging" artists can get a fair shake—despite what they advertise. The panels are generally composed of self-serving glad-handers. Rarely will you see people contradict each other (unless I'm on one of the panels), and it's very hard to extract any useful info unless you know how to read between the lines of what's being said.

This is the dark side, however—one that needs to be tempered with a bit of optimism. Since this business is about connections, you need to make as many as you can. Given this, I'd say it's better to go to one high-end conference than several low-end ones. MIDEM first, if you can afford it, then SXSW. The rest are probably a waste of time in terms of trying to "get a deal." But they provide other value, mostly in terms of building social equity—a fancy sociology term for acquiring lots of important friends. Some economists rank social equity higher in value than actual money or power.

I surveyed many of my industry advisors for this question and got back a uniform answer from my over-40 veterans. "A conference is a great time to catch up with people you talk to on the phone all year, but don't get to see." There you have it. It's a reunion. Now ask yourself this question: Can you get a great deal or make a great contact if you go to someone else's high school reunion? Maybe. But it's not going to be easy.

If conferences are really just a way to network with people you know, then you'll have to know the right angle and find a way into an existing clique without looking creepy. Shoving your product in a veteran's face is the easiest way to be forgotten. My best advice is to have a unique plan. Don't talk about how your band is the best. Offer something of value to the connections you're trying to make. One day you'll be the veteran sitting at a lunch table with all the people you survived with up to that point, and some twentysomething who has barely done a few demos will want to eat with you. Imagine how you'll feel at that moment.

So, which conferences should you go to? The next section provides what accountants call a cost/benefit analysis. It compares the cost of going to a conference with the potential yield in social equity. Make a friend = make a deal. That's the motto of any large gathering of like-minded folk. Live it.

Should I Stay or Should I Go Now? Which Conferences Are Really Worth It?

There are literally over 100 music business conferences in the US and Canada *each year*! Most are so small you've never heard of them. Page 61 contains a cost/benefit analysis of some of the more well-known ones.

The "average cost" number is based on surveys of over 54 music biz veterans, and is an aggregate number that includes admission fees, airfare, hotel, a self-imposed per diem of about $75 a day, and the cost of the materials one generally needs to bring (press kits, cards, flyers, etc.). If the conference is in a major city, the cost presumes airfare. All presume mid-priced hotels for the amount of days that the conference lasts.

The column called "SEY" stands for "Social Equity Yield." This is a (1–10) rating based on how much influential juice you can potentially aggregate compared to the cost of taking off work and flying to the conference. It's weighted toward those US-based artists (or their managers/producers, etc.) looking to connect with higher-ups who can get them noticed, signed, endorsed, etc. Location plays a big role. Conferences in Nashville, Los Angeles, and New York fare higher in this system, since you can network outside of the conference hub while in each city. Other factors include what level of executive is in *general attendance* (disregarding people like keynote speakers and panelists, or if you're attending as a vendor), and size: If the conference is small and cheap, but there are "X" number of potential hot contacts to be made, the SEY will be higher than for a large conference with just as many targets. Lastly, there is the "swinging dick" factor. If you're a guitar player looking for session work, do you want to go to a a Guitar Expo conference of only guitar players? No. You always want to be the most unique person in the room. For this reason, conferences like Sundance rank high. You'll be in a room full of filmmakers. When do they ever need music?

Anything below a 6 rating is a "good-time" write-off. As you might expect, you tend to get what you pay for in this chart, with some surprising exceptions.

Name of Conference	Average Cost	SEY	Comments
SXSW (South by Southwest)	$5,000	6	You'll wait in line more than anything else. Lots of top execs if you can find them in the massive crowds.
CMJ (College Music Journal)	$3,000	5	College radio people. Good for making promo inroads.
NAMM (National Association of Music Merchants)	$1,000	5	Imagine Guitar Center on steroids. Lots of gear, but too many people to navigate effectively.
MIDEM (Marché International du Disque et de l'Edition Musicale)	$10,000	10	Rich hotties and their sugar daddies. Good hunting for cash, if you've already got plenty of your own.
WMC (Winter Music Conference)	$3,000	4	DJ and dance music hookups. Great drugs and beach scene.
ASCAP EXPO	$1,500	8	Songwriters galore. If you need to meet songwriters, go here. Great mentor sessions with top pros make it worth the price of admission.
AES (Audio Engineering Society)	$1,500	4–7, depending	Geeks who never date. Good if you're looking for an internship at a recording studio or want to meet producers who are gear shopping.
Eurosonic	$7,000	5	The SXSW of Europe. A blast, but it's very far away.
FMC (Future of Music Coalition)	$1,500	4	Meet egghead constitutional authorities who argue about whether or not music should be free.
Billboard Music & Money Symposium	$2,000	8	Meet some name-brand music lawyers. You probably can't afford them, but it's good to be in touch with them and know who they are. A good investment.
Billboard Film & TV Music Conference	$4,000	9	Music supervisors. Best value on the page for those with finished masters for licensing.
NARM (National Association of Recording Merchandisers)	$6,000	8	A great backdoor way to meet label people on the marketing side. Managers galore.
NARAS functions	$500	8	Small, intimate gatherings that often have marquee speakers. Good opportunity for those with the gift of gab.

Name of Conference	Average Cost	SEY	Comments
AMBC (AustralAsian Music Business Conference)	$10,000	5	Too far away to seriously consider.
ABA (American Bar Association) Sport and Entertainment Division	$5,000	4–9, depending	The top lawyers are all there, but they don't want to talk to creators. They want to bitch about them to each other. I give it a 4, unless you are climbing the legal ladder; then it's a 9.
TAXI Road Rally	$700	7.5	Meet more undiscovered and unpublished songwriters than you ever thought existed. It's free, so that artificially inflates the score on the left from a 6.
MUSEXPO	$2,000	8	The UN of music conferences. Executive hunting ground. European meet 'n' greet.
West Coast Songwriters Conference	$1,000	5	Songwriter coffee klatch. TAXI Jr.
Digital Music Forum East & West	$2,000	5	Geek fest. Best to only go if you can program in C++ or better.
SGA(Songwriters Guild of America)	$800	5	Old timers. Not worth it.
Pollstar Live!	$3,000	9	Venue promoters. Get on a better tour. Meet managers of top acts. Often overlooked.
Sundance Film Festival	$7,000	10	Be one of the only music people in the room. Bring lots of cash and fun toys. Network with tomorrow's Christopher Nolan or Spielberg. Pricey but worth it.
Hollywood Reporter	$4,000	8	Well networked. Very good speakers who are accessible. Attracts more doers than wannabes.
LAMC (Latin Alternative Music Conference)	$2,000	7	Small but potent. If you're Latin, you have to go. If you're not Latin and want to meet someone who is, make sure you speak Spanish before you buy a ticket.
Digital Hollywood	$2,500	8	Lots of suites with ponytails. Good hunting for just about everything.

Below are a few LA-based non-conferences. By that I mean they are not annual big events, but monthly soirées. You don't hear about them often, but you can do a great deal of damage with these little luncheons.

Name of Conference	Cost	SEY	Comments
CCC (California Copyright Conference)	$75; meets monthly	8	Top publishers and lawyers in abundance.
AIMP (Association of Independent Music Publishers)	$75; meets monthly	9	Publishers. Except for the super biggies, every decent publishing exec is there. Go sell a song.
BHBA (Beverly Hills Bar Association)	$100; meets monthly	7	Lawyers. We all need them. You DO NOT have to be a lawyer or member to attend.
NYBA (New York Bar Association)	$100; meets monthly	7	Same as above in New York.

The Basics of How to Work a Music Conference

➔Don't shove your CD/press kit or data file in the face of everyone you meet. Especially any execs you may bump into. They get tons of this stuff, and believe me, they end up leaving many of these CDs in their hotel rooms. Instead, make a connection. I always tell my garage band clients, "Make a friend and you will make a deal." Exchange cards; make a connection on a personal level. Then follow up in a week or two.

➔Expect most of what you hear on panels to be at best half-truths and at worst totally false. Do not ever rely on information told to you by a multiperson panel. They tend to be fronting.

➔ Don't be too hard on yourself. If you walk away from a conference making only two really, really solid connections, you did OK.

➔ The real action is in the green room. If you can find an excuse to get back there, you'll make better hookups. But don't stalk outside like a weird fan.

➔ The second best place to hook up is the bar.

➔ Remember the golden rule of all business: You have to give to get. Don't be stingy with your money. If somebody is selling something they created, take an interest in it. If it's not too expensive, buy it. You'll make a friend. Make a friend = make a deal.

➔ Most important communication technique: Don't be interesting; be interested. If you find that you're using the word "I" more than twice in a 15-minute conversation, you're probably being narcissistic. Learn about the other person and take a real interest in them.

➔ In case you missed it, make a friend = make a deal.

Contribution thanks to Dan Kimpel, educator, journalist, and author of Networking Strategies for the New Music Business. *A must read.*

Are CDs Dead? When Will Digital Sales Make Up the Majority of Revenue?

CDs are far from dead, and will not be extinct till at least 2020. People who compare CDs to cassettes or vinyl are not taking into consideration one important factor: those platforms are dead or outmoded because cassette players are not manufactured very much any more (or turntables, for that matter). By comparison, every day 100,000 new CD players are manufactured in the form of Xbox players, DVD players, and car stereos. Each of these is backward-compatible with the CD format. This will extend the life of the CD far into the foreseeable future.

Also, real music fans are acutely aware that CDs are capable of archiving their favorite music. Aside from their collectable value, they preserve the original 44.1 kHz, 16-bit recording. In comparison, MP3 and AAC files are not great audio quality. Sure, they sound fine on earbuds or computer speakers, but home systems are getting better and better each year, and the demand for better audio quality will only increase.

Also, digital stores regularly upgrade their file standards, which requires music buyers to continually upgrade. Yes, it's true—that song you paid 99 cents for today will likely not be playable a decade from now. At least not easily. You'll have to buy it in a new format. (If you think otherwise, I got a closet full of 78 rpm records to sell you.) Yet if you have a CD you can just reburn it, practically forever.

When will digital revenue overtake CD sales? It's hard to say precisely. In some countries it already has. Several European countries have reported a complete absorption.

In the US the process will take longer because we're so damn big. Many experts were very sure that it would have already happened by now. But they didn't take into account the factors above. My guess is that by 2015 CD sales will level off at about 350 million units a year in the US and stay there for quite some time; meanwhile, digital downloads and streams will surpass CDs in revenue, not because of actual unit sales, but because of the ad revenue that sites will be sharing with labels. While physical sales stall at about $3.5 billion a year, virtual sales will catch up to about the same amount around 2015.

So, by 2015 we'll see a consumer sales index for direct music sales (CDs, streams, downloads, ringtones, etc.) of about $7 billion a year. In other music sales, licensing will make up the balance of another $3 billion, so we will basically be a $10-billion-a-year industry. Which is about the same gross revenue that the music biz had in the year 2000 in the US.[3]

However, this does not provide the entire picture. Since overhead will be radically reduced, we will be a far leaner industry. This means we'll be squeezing more juice from the proverbial lemon. Without getting into fancy accounting terminology, it means that we as an industry will be making more profit from the $10 billion we will be earning in 2015 than we did with the $10 billion we earned in 2000. Bottom line, we will be better off. More money will flow into more pockets. Superstars and the infrastructure that profits from them—managers, lawyers, etc., will still complain that the business is "dying." This is because we will be spreading the same amount of money into more hands, and it's coming

---

3. RIAA charts show that US music business revenue was $16 billion in 1999–2000, but this is based on anecdotal data that included estimates on units shipped, as opposed to units actually sold over the counter, plus some revenue that should not have been counted in the first place, like PRO data. Today's RIAA statistics are better segregated, but are still biased for other reasons. Regardless, these are still the best general publicly available guidelines we have for tracking US recorded music business revenue.

The $10 Billion Dollar Music Pyramid.

Disbursement of Recorded Music Revenue in 2010

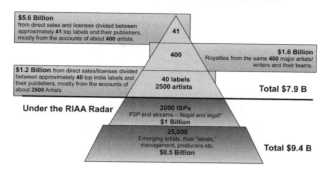

$5.6 Billion from direct sales and licenses divided between approximately **41** top labels and their publishers, mostly from the accounts of about **400** artists.

41

400

$1.6 Billion Royalties from the same **400** major artists/writers and their teams.

$1.2 Billion from direct sales/licenses divided between approximately **40** top indie labels and their publishers, mostly from the accounts of about **2500** Artists.

40 labels
2500 artists

Total $7.9 B

Under the RIAA Radar

2000 ISPs
P2P and streams – illegal and legal*
$1 Billion

25,000
Emerging artists, their "labels," management, producers etc.
$0.5 Billion

Total $9.4 B

More entities with only a slight reduction in revenue creates a perceived "depression."
The difference in total 10-year loss, including "under the radar" is only $200 million (less than 2%).

* This is diverted money earned by P2P sites such as Kazzaa, LimeWire, and hundreds of others. It also includes legal sales of used CDs.

Disbursement of Recorded Music Revenue in 1999-2000

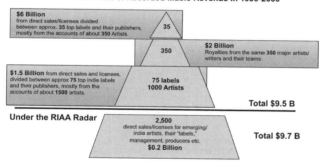

$6 Billion from direct sales/licenses divided between approx. **35** top labels and their publishers, mostly from the accounts of about **350** Artists.

35

350

$2 Billion Royalties from the same **350** major artists/writers and their teams.

$1.5 Billion from direct sales and licenses, divided between approx **75** top indie labels and their publishers, mostly from the accounts of about **1500** artists.

75 labels
1000 Artists

Total $9.5 B

Under the RIAA Radar

2,500
direct sales/licenses for emerging/indie artists, their "labels," management, producers etc.
$0.2 Billion

Total $9.7 B

This chart and two that follow show how both the disproportionate allocation of wealth and reallocation of existing revenue can create a perceived "depression" in the music space.

Probable Disbursement of Recorded Music Revenue in 2025
(not adjusted for inflation)

$6.3 Billion from direct sales/licenses, new SX revenue, divided between approximately **25** top labels, their one-deep subsidiaries, and their publishers from the accounts of about **850*** artists.

25

850

$1.7 Billion Royalties from the same **850** major artists/writers and their teams.

New Rights Aggregators
$1.3 Billion Internet/digital related royalties*

Total $9.3 B

Under the RIAA Radar

40,000
Indie artists, their "labels," and their teams
$1.2 Billion: direct sales/licenses

Total $10.5 B

The pyramid base widens, spreading revenue more evenly.
Indie artists make more on a per-artist basis.
Major label artists will make less on the same basis.

* label consolidation will put many more artists under one roof.
* This is money paid from ISPs, digital transmissions, and ad-based revenue, most of which existed and was under the radar or otherwise un-realized before 2010.

mostly out of *their* pockets. Spreading the base of the pyramid means the top is less heavy. I guess they will just have to learn to live with only one Lear Jet. (See charts on previous page for how the $10 billion pyramid works.)

What Are the Pros and Cons of Working with a Publishing Company? Should I Just Start My Own?

Yes! If you're a songwriter, definitely start your own publishing company. There is not a single disadvantage to it, except that you'll have to file tax forms that will set you back a few bucks each year. But the trade-off is well worth it, especially when it comes time to answering the first part of this question, "What are the pros and cons of working with a publisher?"

If you have already assigned publishing rights to a publisher (even if it's your own company), then larger publishers will only be able to do a "co-publishing deal" with you. This means, very simply, that you'll be in a better negotiating position, so you don't have to sign over the copyright to the other publisher. This is always good for you.

The pros of doing a co-publishing deal with a publisher are as follows:

➜ It adds professionalism and legitimacy to your work.

➜ You don't have to become a collection agency. What—you think people just willingly hand over the cash they owe you for using your music? Nah; they often need gentle persuasion. A letter from Warner Chappell's Legal Affairs department goes a long way toward getting your money versus an e-mail with a yahoo suffix.

➜ Connections. The publisher will probably have more than you, and will get your song in front of more prospective buyers.

➜Time. You can now go play poker all day, knowing that someone else is handling your business.

Cons: There are only two, really.

➜You're giving up a large percentage. Between 35%–70%.

➜Commitment. If you don't like the way the publisher is handling your account, there is not much you can do about it until the contract ends. That is why you should try to keep terms short, until they prove themselves.

Why the Heck Is Music Publishing So Arcane and Hard to Explain to Anyone?

Probably because the nature of publishing itself has changed a lot in the past 30 years. Once it was about song development and placement. To this degree, it was also about brokering the material to artists and then collecting the money the song earned. Legal teams were necessary for collection, as well as teams of songwriters and demo producers to hammer out versions of songs for each artist that was interested in a particular song in the publisher's catalog. It was a vital machine in the heyday of music publishing (1940s). The standard deal back then was that in exchange for a healthy advance (or in many cases a salary), writers would assign the copyright of their work to the publisher, who was charged with exploiting, collecting, and protecting the work. The publisher's take for all this was between 35% and 50%, depending on the bargaining power of the writer.

But the Internet, the devaluation of some rights, and the concept of "debt financing" has changed the publishing business.

Starting around the mid-'60s you had the development of the Artist/Writer. Today this model is a given, but once upon a time it was rare for artists to write their own material.

Sure, an artist might write a song or two here and there, but songwriters were a separate breed, and the publishing company represented their rights.

But labels, which generally wish to pay songwriters as little as possible, saw an opportunity in the 1960s. The public began to view an artist who sang his own songs as somehow more genuine. As soon as "genuineness" became a higher priority than, say, looks or singing ability, labels figured out that it was far easier to make a bad singer sound acceptable with studio trickery than it was to make a bad song a hit. So they started signing songwriters as artists, but only if the songwriters gave them a break on the license for recording their songs. Which most all of them did. Writers now didn't need publishing companies to be brokers, since they were recording their own material. So publishing companies became little more than collection agents.

Then in the 1980s, the concept of *debt financing* reached the music space. This is what Wall Street does when they leverage the value of a company at many times its earnings and then borrow money against that inflated value. If you saw the movie with Michael Douglas then you get the idea. A large infusion of capital is given to the company in exchange for the right to collect against its earnings. This is great as long as assets continue to earn more and more cash.

Now, publishing companies began to view their revenue streams of hit songs as "futures." Meaning that you could get people to invest in a song's future earnings the same way you could buy a position on soybeans or pork bellies on the Commodities Exchange, speculating whether the price would go up or down.

Publishing companies became investment bankers—or, I should say, hired Wall Street firms to leverage their catalogs with outrageous multiples. For every dollar a song earned today, a bank would advance them $5 or $10 for the right to collect that revenue for the next 10 years. Almost none of the new money went to the writers. It was not considered "earnings," but a loan made to the publisher and a debt burden on the copyright itself. But as long as the value of the song was going up, no one worried.

This worked fine for until 2009, when the financial crisis devalued most things that were packaged as a security. Mortgage-backed securities, as well as song income, took a dive. "Bowie Bonds," as they were called (because David Bowie was one of the first to leverage his publishing into investor-grade bonds), began to drop. Loans were called in, with interest—devaluing the catalogs. So publishing companies had to return to their old model of selling songs and collecting revenue from the sales of music. Just one problem—since most of their revenue (and valuation) was based on CD sales, they were screwed, since CD sales were in freefall from 2000–2009. Revenue from CD sales (called mechanicals) slipped by almost 30% between 2001 and 2009, and Wall Street learned the hard way that investing in songs was far riskier than it thought.

Does any of this explain what publishing is? No, but it gives you an idea of why it has gotten so complicated to explain exactly what a publisher does. Tomorrow's publisher will likely be returning to its roots. I think the days of hit-song-backed securities are about over. But you never know. Recently, record companies have gained new ground in getting Congress to establish rates so radio and TV stations can start paying performance royalties for the sound recording. (This system already exists in most other parts of the world. Just not in the US, due to the influence of broadcasters.) If the RIAA succeeds, then we'll see a huge new resurgence in sound recording *publishing*. Let's see if they can convince Wall Street to loan them 10 cents on the penny for Pink Floyd and Bob Dylan recordings. Stay tuned.

All the reasons above are why I say that one should think of a song's publishing the same way they would think of stock in a company. It's not about who writes the song. It's about who has a financial interest in it.

What Is a Good First Publishing Deal?

A Four-Album Deal with a Major Label

Any deal involving multiple albums in my opinion requires you to consider that label's publishing division as a first choice. Exceptions would be:

→ If the label is small and their pub division has little or no infrastructure.

→ If the advance sucks.

→ If you get a better offer elsewhere.

A good trade-off for working with your label's publisher would mean a full statutory rate and payment on 90% of all records *shipped*—not all records sold—and no reserves.

(If you don't understand that sentence, consult my other books, *Confessions of a Record Producer* and *Secrets of Negotiating a Record Contract*.)

Publishing Deals with Production Companies

When producers/writers sign writers to their publishing companies, how are these deals worked out with the writers?

When signing to big producers as a sub-producer/writer, you can expect to make substantially less than in a traditional publishing deal on a major label. Often production companies take an additional service fee for taking a chance on you that is tantamount to about 25%. This is not specific to any particular company, but is what almost everyone does.

Generally a writer for a production company makes about 30 cents per dollar earned. That's fairly common. The company collects *all* the money on such deals, much like a record deal, and uses it to offset expenses incurred on "your behalf." You get the rest several months later.

If you check out my second book, *Secrets of Negotiating a Record Contract*, I go into many numbers on how these deals tie into a recording contact.

As a songwriter, should I go under contract with a small publisher (who claims to have a major label contact), a large publisher, or try co-publishing with a producer?

I would almost NEVER recommend a co-pub deal with a for-hire producer. The exception is if the producer is very highly accredited. (This should not be confused with "sharing" your publishing with a producer in lieu of them charging you for their work. That is a different question entirely.)

One has to remember why you sign a pub deal in the first place. It's because the entity you are giving your rights to has the clout to collect the money you are owed all over the world. Can a local producer do that? Doubtful. Can a small publisher? Doubtful, even if they have a major contact. What kind of contact do they have, anyway? How is it connected to the collection of publishing income?

These are all legitimate questions to ask before you sign.

What's the Difference Between ASCAP, BMI, and SESAC? Which One Should I Join?

Here's a rock 'n' roll answer: How about none of them.

All of these competing Performing Rights Organizations (PROs) spend a great deal of their members' money selling "belonging" as if there is an immediate benefit to membership. The truth is that you can only get money from one of these organizations if you have music that is being publicly performed many, many, many, many times in very, very, very public places: in a major motion picture, on a network TV broadcast, TV show theme song, or in constant rotation on a major radio station.

ASCAP (American Society of Composers, Authors and Publishers) and BMI (Broadcast Music, Inc.) will both tell you it is irrational *not* to join one of their organizations. They collect the bulk of all the performance royalties in the US, and you cannot get your share unless you are a member. In their pitch they will make it sound as if your music is already out there earning money and the PRO is just holding it for you, like a bank, waiting for your application. But the truth is that unless you wrote a popular song or composed a soundtrack for a TV show like *The Simpsons* you are unlikely to see any significant royalties, even if you are a member.

Regardless, I'd have to say that, under the right circumstances, joining a PRO is wiser than not joining one. For practicality, the real question is not *should* you join, but *when* and *which one* should you join. Many people who are new to the industry think they should sign up as soon as they can. The lavish events that both ASCAP and BMI host make one think that joining means there is an *immediate* chance to collect money. I'm not so sure this is true. Even if you are a member, you only get paid if:

1. There is money to collect for *your* musical works and, more important . . .

2. If you meet their requirements to receive money *after* you join.

This means it's entirely possible that after you commit to a PRO, your song(s) could be earning money for your PRO, but the PRO is paying you *nothing in return*. So, unless one offers you a financial incentive, I don't see this choice as a real dilemma until and unless you have written music that fits one of the following criteria:

➔ It was recorded by a significant artist and the album or single is about to be released.

➔ It was placed in a movie soundtrack that is about to be broadcast on a major TV network.

➔ It was used as a theme for a series that is about to be broadcast on a significant TV network.

➔ It is currently getting *a lot* of play on a *commercial* radio station or podcast, or it has been tracked by a reliable service as being downloaded (legally) thousands of times.

Notice that all four items above are happening *now* or about to happen in the *near* future; not things that have happened in the past or will happen in a year or two. Both ASCAP and BMI have payout systems that tend to respect events that are *around the corner*. If you had a hit five years ago and are just thinking about joining now or you've just been signed to a major label but you haven't even recorded your first album yet, don't expect to have any real negotiating leverage. Also notice what's NOT on my list above—writing the music for:

➔ A TV commercial.

➔ A soundtrack for a movie that has only seen theatrical or direct-to-video distribution in the US.

➔ Independent films that show at festivals *only*.

➔ A hot regional artist's indie release.

For reasons that are too lengthy to go into here (but are discussed in detail in my other book, *Confessions of a Record Producer*), these circumstances tend to not track on either ASCAP's or BMI's systems. However, any of the bottom four could someday metamorphose into the top four. If so, which PRO you join could make a radical difference in your income. Since joining is really the only bargaining chip you have, I say wait a bit, and see which way the wind blows for your career.

As for the differences, they are subtle, but significant. Each PRO has an accounting system that favors different types of public performances. Both ASCAP and BMI will tell you that they pay the same, because to admit otherwise would get them into a bit of trouble with the law. But this "we pay the same" pitch is a very transparent lie to catch them in. Because if a representative of ASCAP knows what BMI pays, they will tell you that they don't know. And vice versa. So how can they tell you they pay the same if they don't know how each other pays?

They cannot, and there have been many cases of songwriter teams who are on competing PROs who have wildly varying checks for the EXACT same song performed in the EXACT same way.

Clearly they do not pay the same.

To my knowledge the only critical analysis of the difference between the Coke and Pepsi of PROs is in the latest edition of my first book, *Confessions of a Record Producer*. If this is still a burning question after the explanation above, then I urge you to read chapter 20 in *Confessions*.

Does Staying Indie Mean I'll Have More Freedom but Less Money? Has Anyone Stayed Indie and Gone Platinum in the US? How Did They Do It?

The short answer to the first part: who knows?

The short answer to the second part: no.

Ani DiFranco is probably the most famous of the truly "indie" artists. She released her records through her own label, Righteous Babe, and steadily built a devout grassroots following on the strength of touring. An ardent feminist and an open bisexual, her songs tackled issues like rape, abortion, and sexism. She is responsible for the restoration of an architectural building and galvanizing the Buffalo arts scene.

But, while touting DiFranco as a hero, few have probably

been to her website and read her own words about how she's enjoying only "modest profits." "I have indeed sold enough records to open a small office on the half-abandoned main street in the dilapidated urban center of my hometown, Buffalo, NY. I am able to hire 15 or so folks to run and constantly reinvent the place while I drive around and play music for people."

She can get away with staying indie because of geography. Her employees live as modestly as students, working more for social equity than cash. Try doing this in LA or New York, and you'll quickly see that the model has wet noodles for legs. DiFranco's determination is admirable, and what she's given back to her community is inescapable, but it's unwise for aspiring artists navigating major metropolitan cities to try to duplicate.

Artists working in urban areas usually can't make a living off music and nothing else. They are able to enjoy the same modest profits that a DiFranco might (and possibly more), but this money will mostly go toward the extras in life. Rent, food, and car bills, normal for Los Angeles or New York, will have to come from some other job, possibly one that is music-related — working for a manager, distributor, or musical instrument store; running a studio, engineering, etc.

The "DiFranco Model" makes sense if your music is so niche that you have no choice but to do the DIY thing. To aspire to her model as an ultimate level of success might be setting your sights a bit low prematurely. Many believe that with the Internet affording people many new opportunities that there will emerge a new business model that will break an artist on a mass scale using the DIY religion. This was being said in 1998 when *Confessions of a Record Producer* came out, and I was criticized for my "doubting Thomas" attitude toward how significant the Internet would be in this regard. It's been over 10 years now, and with the exception of Tila Tequila, and possibly OneRepublic (if you can consider them "indie" since they signed with an Interscope imprint), I'm still in the black on this prediction. But on an indie level the Internet is an invaluable marketing tool that is maturing every day.

To me the old formulas are still the best ones. Become a local success. Use that as a platform to spread your wings. Work social networks toward that goal. When you can't think of another way to make money within a 50-mile radius of your house, get a booking agent and start thinking about getting on a national tour.

Everyone I know who has made a living off of music has followed more or less the same path. Those oddball stories you read about where someone becomes a YouTube sensation and gets a multi-album deal on a major label are largely urban legends.

Does the Public Really Prefer Singles to Albums?

This is an outstanding and sophisticated question. You'd think the answer would be very simple, based on everything you've probably read recently: Singles, of course. You hear story after story of people stealing singles off the Internet, but how many stories do you read about people stealing CDs from record stores?

Well, like most things, when you drill down to the facts, the answer is not as simple as you might think. A better analogy might be if you had two outdoor bins and one had CD singles and one had CD albums, and if nobody was watching, which bin would be emptied out quicker due to theft?

Ah . . . rephrased this way, the answer seems a bit more gray. And it is.

The only really good market research surveys seem to suggest that people enjoy buying more than one song at a time, and it makes sense that if they are going to buy several songs by the same artist, then it should be in an album. An "album" being about 12 songs of similar style and texture assembled in a group.

A bit of history here is important. Up until 1976, albums were a product of convenience. Everyone bought singles unless they were real fans of the artist. Then, in 1962, labels started introducing collections of singles on one large "long-playing" record, called an LP. But in 1967 the Beatles changed the game forever. With the release of *Sgt. Pepper's Lonely Hearts Club Band* the "concept album" was born. This meant that songs were not just grouped in any old order, but that there was a particular flow, and the album was a full 40-minute listening experience, or at least two 20-minute listening experiences, one for each side of the LP. This idea took off, and soon you had albums like *Dark Side of the Moon, Tommy, Jesus Christ Superstar* and many other albums that were each somewhat interactive.

Artists loved concept albums because it meant that they got paid more publishing money (for reasons too complex to go into here[4]). Labels initially were not as excited, because it made marketing a "hit single" more difficult. They preferred the interchangeability of each three-minute song. That way they could create different versions of the albums for different overseas markets.

But soon both ideologies found a way to live together. Artists made sure that at least one or two songs on the album could live independently of the album's concept, and labels realized that most artists (Pink Floyd notwithstanding) didn't have the creative juice to churn out concept album after concept album.

With the "singles market" revitalized again due to iTunes and P2P, the public will get to decide which format they really want. For the first time in history the packaging of music will be decided by the consumers instead of being dependent on business decisions made by accountants, managers, or even artists.

The votes so far seem to be a split decision. As soon as iTunes began to offer albums, people began to buy them with almost the same fervor as singles. In the coming years, labels in turn are going to begin insisting that certain new acts be sold in digital stores as "album only" for the first few months. In 2008 AC/DC and Kid Rock, two of that year's

---

4. For a great analysis of why this is, see *FutureHit.DNA* by Jay Frank.

biggest rock acts, insisted on "album-only" sales in iTunes and other digital stores. Did this insistence pay off? Kid Rock's *Rock N Roll Jesus* was one of the top five albums of that year. It remained available in CD form for almost a year before a digital license was granted. And AC/DC's *Black Ice* album was released exclusively at Wal-Mart, and was trailing right behind Kid Rock's as the fourth best-selling album of 2008, with 1.6 million copies sold, and not one of them a single or a download.

Of course, for every one of these stories there are 100 others who relied on singles sales and digital downloads as the mainstay of their release. But the examples above prove that people still want albums and still want them in CD form. But some marketing and retail experts feel that Rock and AC/DC left a lot of money on the table by standing proudly behind a format that is steadily moving into a museum.

The consensus also seems to feel that this type of move is only achievable by larger acts with very strong followings. A newer act wouldn't dare experiment with this type of strategy. Singles are always going to be part of the marketing strategy of every album. So artists will be compelled to create them out of commercial necessity. The real casualty is the concept album, which already is an endangered species.

Albums *do* sell if they are good. But is this a new lesson? Labels and artists have known this for decades. Also, the entire music business economy is based on the album configuration. Publishing advances are inextricably designed around albums. Can you imagine trying to negotiate a publishing advance when the label says, "We're not going to print any CD albums; just post a couple of singles on digital stores"? Absurd! There would be nothing to base the advance upon. No advances means no flow of capital, and most of us who passed high school economics know what that means. (BTW, I failed that class.)

Another reason CD albums will survive for quite some time? Albums are cool! It's a cohesive, 50-minute sound vision. Singles were created as an economic reality of selling albums, not as a substitute for them. Technology innovators like Steve Jobs don't care about the integrity of music. No human who invented the best way to buy, catalog, and steal individual tracks can be a real fan of modern music! I remember trying to get my mother to join the iPod generation by telling her that it could hold her entire classical collection. She responded, "But it cuts up the symphony into little bits. You're not supposed to listen to a symphony that way." (iTunes used to treat movements like singles and wouldn't play them seamlessly.)

I was ashamed. My aging mother "got it" before I did: music is about creativity, not the technology you play it on. Anyone who tries to tell you otherwise is a music hater, even if they don't know it. They have sold their souls to the tech gods if they truly believe that artists should start making three-minute singles and forget about their album vision just because it's more convenient.

Music lives! Albums live! And for now, the sales numbers prove it.

Why Don't Radio Stations Play Unsigned Acts? Why Can't You Get on Radio Without Major Label Backing?

Since the dawn of rock 'n' roll in the '50s, record companies have known that radio is what breaks a record to the public. In the '60s, many stations consolidated, thereby creating a situation where there were fewer stations and thus less airtime. As with all supply-and-demand situations, competition (in this case the fight to get a song on the air) became intense, and the battle was fought with the major players' sharpest wits.

To outgun their competition, record companies hired independent promoters to "push" certain artists to the radio stations for a good position in the station's rotation (i.e., the list of songs currently being played). Why a station would cooperate with this system is simple to understand. It makes most of its money off advertising—selling products between the songs. In order to charge a lot of money for advertising, a station must have a large listenership. In order to have a large listenership, it has to play the most popular songs. But how can a radio station know that a new artist is going to be popular? It can't, but it can figure out how much exposure a new artist will get by the amount the record label is willing to spend on the artist's promotion.

This type of promotion is very expensive. But that was all right with the labels; keeping the service expensive made it inaccessible to their main competition—the small indie labels and mostly the average garage band.

The practice of using independent promoters is hard for high-level artists to accept. They work for years to develop their sound and songs, and whether they become famous or have to go back to working in a warehouse all depends on some wiseguy in loud clothing, chomping on a huge cigar, greasing a program director with a bribe. No wonder so many artists take drugs!

Despite some recent episodes of a crackdown, such as by New York's ex attorney general, Elliot Spitzer, the indie promoter schmooze has not died out. But it has taken on new forms. In the old days the major indie promoters (not to be confused with indie record labels) were, for the most part, tied to the Mob. As the Mob's interest in the record business thinned out in the late '80s (due to sales buy-outs by multinational conglomerates) and as competition from new, more legitimate promotion companies sprang up, these grifters of radio promotion found new marks.

Labels were slapped with large fines and, as a result, now let the artists hire the independent promoters themselves. Even though it means more work for the artist, it also means that the artist has a bit more control over his or her career and expenses. In lieu of spending the big bucks on promoters, record companies are now free to come up with clever legal ways to promote their records.

Although record companies tend to be very secretive about which promotion scams work and which ones don't, I believe in the Abe Lincoln philosophy, which goes (and I'm paraphrasing), "You can make most of the people buy a crappy record some of the time, and you can make some of the people buy a crappy record most of the time, but you can't make most of the people buy a crappy record most of the time." Basically, you can't make enough people buy a record they hate no matter how much money you throw at it. Although it sure seems that major labels try.

For those of you who have ever wondered why mainstream radio doesn't play your favorite underground or indie band, you should now understand: It's because their label doesn't allocate the money to bribe the right people to play it. So the next time one of your relatives tells you that you should be a singer because your voice is so much better than "the junk on the radio," you can now explain to Aunt Sophie that it isn't that simple. For more on this, see the payola question, page 123.

Where Should I Tour, and How Do I Get Booked?

You should try to get on the biggest tour you can afford. Now, that might not be as simple as it sounds. Touring is more expensive than recording, and just as necessary. Yet very few artists I know reserve very much money for touring. They shoot their load in the studio.

If you're reading this section of the book, then you're at the level where a real tour that produces the best results for you is not opening for a large national act. It's picking a tour of about 300 miles and hitting each club along that route. So, if you're in California, tour the route from Los Angeles to Sacramento. If you're in New York, tour from the Big Apple to Poughkeepsie.

This is how you become a local sensation. Repetition of the same clubs every six to 10 months. At each venue you make friends, hang out with the locals, and sell, sell, sell merchandise.

When you're at the next level of your career, that is the time to get a serious sponsor and let them pay the fees to get you opening in front of a national act. (See the question on touring budgets, page 116.) Even then you will probably only be able to afford to follow them for a single leg of their tour. When this happens the best strategy is to have a small piece of that leg overlap the region where you live/already know people. You'll get all your fans showing up at their show. This is good business for everyone.

Can You Get Discovered on the Internet, and Will You Make Good Money Because People Hear You on YouTube?

If the RIAA (Recording Industry Association of America) and the NMPA (National Music Publishers Association) are successful in getting ISPs to start paying real money for the performance of YouTube plays, then yes, even a garage band with no major label affiliation will start making significant cash from YouTube and similar services.

However, this day may be several years away—if ever. But when it comes I can see a day in the not too distant future when YouTube (or an independent company) tracks the number of plays on a given video and pays about 1/10 of a cent per play. If you've got something that plays 1,000,000 times, you'll earn a gross of $1,000. And that's just for one service. If you're getting 1,000,000 plays on YouTube, you're probably getting equal amounts elsewhere, which will lead to licensing deals that are far more lucrative.

There are also fees that are presently being negotiated with larger ISPs for a blanket license to cover illegal P2P file sharing.

No one knows yet what these fees will look like, but you know whatever they are that it will add up to real money someday. I'm guessing in the hundreds of millions a year.

How Much Can I Make If I Stay Indie?

If your goal is to be pop diva à la Lady Gaga, then you have no real options. You must sign with a major label or one of their closely held affiliates (which I call One-Deep Labels, from the *Confessions of a Record Producer*'s Hierarchy of Labels Chart). The pop sensation machinery has not really been altered by new technology. You still need the basic components of a major label/management/production vehicle.

However, if you're not thinking about playing 20,000-seat arenas four nights a week for 30 weeks a year, then your options greatly open up. You probably don't need a production company at all. You can hire a producer, and instead of signing a five-year management contact that gives up 20% of your gross, you can hire a consultant for an interim period. Top pros can be had for a monthly fee that is far cheaper in the long run than a manager. And best of all, you can fire them any time you want.

As for how much you can make this way, I have a few thoughts. I have several clients who are middle-class recording artists. They are not famous outside of their fan base. They will probably never have a hit record. But they play 100 colleges a year, every year, and some do nothing but play folk festivals. They move about 5,000 CDs a year at about $12 each. They pull in about $300,000 a year gross. After they pay everyone they are left with a net of about $200,000, which they divide four ways. Not a bad way to make a living. They keep small apartments or a house that they only live in a few months out of the year. They rent it out when they are out of town and own very little in the way of what George Carlin called "stuff."

This is easily doable, but there is a downside. You cannot

do it forever. What keeps these cats up at night is how they can build on their past so that they can scale it outwards. This is very tough. Without some form of a hit you can keep touring past 40ish.

Most of these guys will eventually split up and start playing as a side player for some other top cats. If they are women, the Vegas odds say they will likely marry and settle down. Some will take their music money and buy a house. But the one thing they all have is a backup plan.

This, like it or not, is an indie success story. If you can do this for 10 years, pay your bills, sock away some cash for the future, and not get hooked on drugs or arrested, in my book and by the law of averages, you're a success.

How Much Money Do I Need to Invest to Make It as an Artist or Producer?

Artist

If you've flipped to this question as one of your first, then odds are you have a better than 50% chance of making it over others who looked at questions like "When do I need a manager?" Why? Because you're addressing the most frustrating but essential part of any career—financial infrastructure. Or, to use an old adage, "You have to put gas in the bus to make it run."

Careers are expensive. Any career. Aside from buying a house, there is not likely to be anything you invest more of your money in than the infrastructure of your career. Doctors and lawyers invest over $150,000 in their education alone. This is usually followed by about $250,000 in basic tools like equipment, reference books, and subscriptions to various necessary professional services.

Many musicians understand this concept of investment when it comes to things like their instruments, studio time, and gear. But try to talk to them about things like education, PR, and bookkeepers, and they quickly start zoning out. Yes, the essential things for business are usually quite boring. But you need them.

How much is too much to spend? That's the question. It's hard to answer, but I can give you a barometer. Prior to about 1995, when I was a producer I used to tell the investors who financed my client's productions that they should be prepared to spend about $60,000. Only $25,000 went into the recording. The rest was all PR and other "boring" things.

Today that number has gone up and not just because of inflation. In 2002 a Wall Street firm put together a fund speculating on recording artists. The fund raised about $10,000,000 to invest in various new acts. Each act was allocated a fund of $300,000. $80,000 was for recording and the rest for the "boring" stuff: PR, marketing, advertising, promotion, outfits, etc. This raised the bar to levels that were unobtainable to most. But that was part of the plan. To outspend the competition and therefore hedge the risk of failure.

It sort of worked. Some artists got bought out and signed to majors; others disappeared. But what this did to the business of artist development was radical. If Wall Street saw the potential in developing artists, that meant that the music business had moved out of the basement and into the boardroom. It also meant bigger players and bigger development budgets.

Several of these funds have come and gone, with various degrees of success, but in their wake they have left a formula

Recording/production	$35,000
Marketing (including Internet, viral marketing, SEO, etc.)	$40,000 ($8,000 a month for five months)
Public relations	$30,000 ($5,000 for six months)
Artist salaries	$100,000 ($500/week for four players for one year)
Equipment/rehearsal	$50,000
Touring	$100,000
Administrative/legal/consulting fees	$38,000
Total	**$393,000**

that is becoming a standard. Above is a table showing what their budget looked like for an 18-month artist development period.

Look at the proportions of creative money to "boring stuff." About 1:4. Major labels follow this same ratio, expecting that their recording budget will be about $250,000 and their bottom line will hover around $1,000,000. Now you don't need to spend this much, but it helps to know that this is what your competition is spending. In my third book, *Million-Dollar Mistakes*, I show that the number-one reason most new acts fail is that they are undercapitalized. They do not spend enough in the right ways.

Producer

Producers fall into a different spending category. Although I've never heard of a hedge fund for speculating on producers, I fail to see why it would make any less financial sense than speculating on artists.

Most of the producer's investment is in gear. While artists look at a 1:4 ratio for creative versus "boring" stuff, the producer's ratio is far more fun. Probably more in the 5:2 range. For every five dollars a producer spends on his studio, he should spend about two dollars on PR, marketing, consulting, etc. This is not a proven formula, but I'm willing to bet it's more generous than most producers, who spend 110% of their money on gear and completely ignore the rest.

The formulas above should act as a guideline, but don't try to do this without some professional advice. This is where a manager or consultant can really earn their fee. Seek professional advice before putting together your business plan and before you begin spending this money.

What Kind of Terms Should Be in a Licensing Agreement?

A licensing deal is one where someone wants to "rent" your music for a specific purpose: a movie soundtrack, TV theme, commercial, website, music library, etc. Often the contracts are no more than a few pages, and there are several standard clauses to look for. These deals are almost never exclusive, especially if there is no great amount of money attached.

Type of License

This explains how the music will be used: as foreground, background, over dialogue, opening credits, etc. And then how many seconds or minutes of the music will appear in the final cut. Each has a negotiation that goes along with it. More time means more money.

Right to Alter

This grants the person paying for the license the right to chop it up to suit their needs. Some artists allow no altering; some are very liberal. It usually depends on the type of use and how much they are being paid.

Length of License

For films the length will almost always be in perpetuity and forever. It's too damn expensive to remove a song from a soundtrack after it's in place. But if it's for anything else, you have some room. Commercial licenses typically last no more than six months. TV, two years. Greeting cards and new media, one to three years.

Territory

What region of the world will the license be for? Believe it or not, a company has often made the mistake of paying big bucks for a song, only to forget to negotiate worldwide rights. They go to the Cannes film festival and get a great European distribution deal for their film, only to discover that they only got the US rights for the music in the film. It happens more often than you think.

All-In Rights

When a film company licenses a piece of music, they do not own the copyright. Only the right to have the music in their new work. When that work is performed publicly, the owners of the copyright get paid still another fee called a "performance fee." That's the fee that is paid for public performance of the music when it's in the movie. This can add up to a great deal of cash, so recently licensing deals have asked authors of works to allocate these rights to the film's producer or production company. Songwriters who belong to ASCAP or BMI are forbidden to sign such deals.

Price

Finally, there is the price for the bundle of rights. There should be some type of stepped fees if you're giving a free or very cheap license. The more valuable the film becomes as a property, the more fees should be paid at each benchmark.

Some famous benchmark licensing deals:

➔ Sony & Cher's "I Got You Babe":
Use in *Groundhog Day*, $88,000 for worldwide rights.
➔ The entire Universal music catalog was licensed to iTunes for about 67% of all revenue for each song downloaded. This license renews every three years.
➔ The Beatles' "Revolution" for a Nike commercial: $9,000,000 for six months; US use only.

And from the "we've come a long way, baby" department:

➔ Sixteen number-one hits from 1951–1961 were licensed to George Lucas for worldwide rights forever, including soundtrack album release rights (something you never get nowadays) for the *American Graffiti* soundtrack in 1971 for a total of $70,000. Today you wouldn't even get 30 seconds of any one of those songs for that amount.

More Questions from Readers on Licensing

I am making a film about a day in the life of a fashion model. During many of the times she recorded footage, radios were playing in the background. Do I need to get clearance for each of these incidental bits of music that someone else was playing in the background as the footage was being recorded?

Yes. It is a common erroneous belief of new film producers that while shooting "documentary"-styled footage, any audio or music caught on tape is "fair use." Not true. It only applies to situations like TV news, when the news team comes busting into a bar or home to get a story and there happens to be a radio or stereo on in the background. The reason this is considered fair use is because requiring the news organization to get a license would inhibit freedom of the press.

The example above is a "made for profit" film where filmmakers are in control of the environment where they shoot. Therefore, you need both a sync *and* a master license for use of the recording in your film.

A toy company would like to use two of my songs to put in a promo toy at their upcoming fair. What should I charge them for using my songs (mind you, they have already been recorded)? Is it a mechanical royalty (9 cents per song) or a flat fee?

You're on the right track. Yes, they should pay you a mechanical royalty. It doesn't matter if the songs have been recorded. It matters if they've been PUBLISHED. If the song has not been published, then you have a lot of leverage over them to negotiate for more money than the statutory 9.1 cents per copy. This information is also covered in both of my books, *Confessions of a Record Producer* and *Secrets of Negotiating a Record Contract*.

However, in the case above a toy company would most likely want to negotiate for an "all-in" style license where they pay a flat fee with bonuses paid at certain benchmarks, rather than a per-unit "mechanical." The fees for the first 5,000 units might be low, but will ramp up quickly after that.

Has the Internet Helped or Hurt the Music Business?

The simple answer: It really depends on who you ask.

Because of the Internet, the playing field is a bit more level between major label acts and indie ones. Promotion costs have gone down considerably, and almost every semi-pro band can afford a $500-a-month SEO person instead of a $3,000-a-month publicist. Social networking makes it possible to aggregate fans with a mouse click, and for the first time you can really be your own distributor. All this, plus Silicon Valley seems to think that the Internet helps *everything*. So that's a two thumbs up for the Internet, right?

Tell that to the thousands of travel and real estate agents who have had to find other careers. Explain to the thousands of people who have degrees in library science that we no longer need as many librarians (or libraries, for that matter), thanks to Google, MSN, and Yahoo.

There is no free lunch.

If you're on the development or IT side of the Internet rage, then it seems like a rosy picture. But if you're part of the "old" way of doing things, where we interfaced with people instead of machines, then you have a different take on it. Think about it: the kind of person who believes that society has progressed because we communicate and make "friends" while sitting alone in a room facing a computer screen is exactly the same type of person who will never understand that popular music is not just about the notes; it's about social awareness and unifying people through a message. It's not just about moving units, but affecting what people think as they are using their purchasing power.

Surely the Internet has injured that. And even if you can make a valid argument that the Internet will ultimately improve the sales of records, you would be hard-pressed to make the argument that it's maintained music's status in our society as a powerful communication medium. No one cares what musicians think anymore. If they criticize the government, they are ridiculed when they were once revered. Music has surely been devalued in that respect. Quite probably into the foreseeable future. (See the last question in the book for more on this.)

As for music sales themselves, has the Internet helped? The jury is still out. We won't know until the dust from the decade-old war between ISPs and content companies reaches a conclusion (which it has not as of this writing, in late 2010), and until the compromises reached as a result are thoroughly integrated into society and then . . . add five years. Then we'll know the answer.

So, in simpler terms: Once ISPs and content companies learn to co-exist peacefully, they will come up with a revenue-sharing plan; one that will incorporate a method of either stopping theft or compensating for it. Once this system (whether it be subscription services, an override, or tax- or ad-based revenue-share) is working (and by working we mean paying everyone ALL the money they are supposed to receive, and then adding a few years on top of that to make sure it's solid), then we can count sales and see if we ever get back to the peak years of 2000 when CD and recorded music sales were at their highest. All in all, give it until about 2020. That's a long time to wait, I know. In the meantime, for your music career you cannot focus on this issue. It's a *force majeure*, an act of nature; it will be what it will be.

We know this: while recorded-music business revenue shrank from a $12 billion-a-year industry to a $9 billion-a-year industry thanks in fair part to illegal P2P file sharing, the amount of revenue that music-related services (illegal and legal) has generated for ISPs has reached over $100 million *a year*, according to some experts. And they won't give us even a little piece of that action. Not a crumb.

So the next time you or one of your friends thinks that the Internet and P2P is cool, remember that someone somewhere is paying for it, and that someone is probably an artist.

PART 3

I'm About to Sign My First *Real* Deal

Questions and Answers for Those Who Have Arrived

Introduction

Hello.

Why am I greeting you when you've probably already been with me for many pages by now? Because even though we've been buddy-buddy for the first two parts of this book, it's the next three parts that will turn you into a pro.

If you've read the table of contents and are interested in the questions in this chapter, it's probably because you've survived the first trial by fire of the music business—getting to the point where you're worthy of making a *real* deal. This also means several other things: it means that you've entered the zone where most people fail and wither back to the ignominy of delivering pizza or going back to school for that accounting degree. Because now that you're good enough to be paid . . .

➜ You're good enough to be ripped off.

➜ You're good enough to want to make it *big*.

➜ You're eager enough to sign something lousy.

➜ You're most certainly an arrogant diva who thinks that she doesn't need to have any business smarts—you'll just get the best lawyer to handle all your problems.

All of these components are a sure-fire formula for ending up in the discount bin and part of VH1's cautionary tale of fallen pop stars, *Behind the Music*. Especially the last point. Without a doubt the number-one reason for artists failing after they work so hard to get their big shot is lack of business knowledge. They think that having a top manager or lawyer is insurance enough to insulate them from disaster. Well, I wrote an entire book filled with stories of how that philosophy can go wrong (*Million-Dollar Mistakes*). Lawyers and managers are a guarantee of only one thing—that you'll pay between 5% and 25% of your money to someone who is doing the job that in many cases you should be doing for yourself.

Sure, there are many exceptions. You need a lawyer and manager to do certain things that you can't while you're creating and touring, but understanding how to protect your rights is your responsibility. If you let someone else watch your back unfettered, you'll end up like some famous cases, such as Billy Joel, who allowed his brother-in-law and his attorney to manage his affairs. The story goes that it cost him millions.

In this chapter we're going to tackle some basic questions that seem like they have simple answers on the surface, but the real answer is somewhat counterintuitive. These are questions that would seem out of reach for a newcomer, but if you've been through at least one deal already—good or bad—you'll see that sometimes the obvious answer is not the correct one.

Let's dive in.

How Can I Tap into Money from Overseas?

What money? Is there money overseas? Oh yeah—a lot of it. In fact, while you could wait years for royalty checks from US labels, there are European agencies that have cash for you now, if you know how to get it.

Neighboring Rights and Sound Recording Public Performance

Unlike the US, just about every other country pays both the record company and the artist for a performance on radio and TV. In the US we only pay the songwriters (this will likely change very soon). The key to getting this sound recording money comes in understanding a term called "Neighboring Rights." As the term implies, this is money for rights that neighboring countries owe to artists, and is collected by Neighboring Rights Organizations (NROs). They are like ASCAP and BMI, except they collect money for the sound recording instead of the composition. One country's radio plays artists from another country. So if a German artist has records playing on French radio, the French NRO collects the money from the French radio stations and pays the German NRO the performance fees. The German NRO in turn pays the artist for their territory.

These new warm and friendly rights are a creation of an international treaty called the Rome Convention, which was adopted in 1961. It protects artists and producers of sound recordings against unauthorized reproduction. It also protects against certain "secondary uses" of music recordings, such as broadcasting. For you this simply means that it creates a revenue stream that must be paid to the producers, labels, and artists of sound recordings when they are played on the radio. Sounds great, right? Where do you sign up?

There's just one problem. The US didn't opt into the Rome Convention. The US and the Soviet Union (Russia) were the only Western world leaders who opted out. The term "neighboring rights" means nothing in the US. We don't pay Canada squat, and they don't pay us either. And since we don't pay European artists for this right when their music is performed here, guess what?— they don't like to pay us either. Instead, we pay digital performing rights for US artists when their music is performed on satellite radio and webcasts with a "digital royalty" that is collected by SoundExchange (www.soundexchange.com). Meanwhile, the European money stays over there.

But there is a workaround.

More and more Canadian and American artists are qualifying for overseas performance monies, and a whole subculture of companies called "royalty recovery agents" has sprung up in recent years that specialize in finding and exploiting these qualifications. These firms can be expensive, often charging rates of 30% and a few grand in upfront fees. But the good news is, you don't need them if you're persistent and have some time on your hands.

One simple action you can do for yourself is to sign up as a US *Artist in Residency* with each NRO. It's time consuming, but can be worth it if you've got music playing anywhere on European TV or radio. Here is a partial list of agencies to contact and register with:

→BREIN
→CEDAR
→IRDA (International Rights Collecting and Distribution Agency)
→MusiCopy
→NORMA
→SENA (Corporation for the Exploitation of Neighbouring Rights)
→VEVAM/SEKAM

You can't simply sign up with one NRO, because unlike ASCAP and BMI and their counterparts in Europe, NROs do not share information with their sister societies or pass on money to a central society as a clearinghouse. Each does its own laundry.

You also have to check in with the NROs every year. Why? Well, because even if they have your money, they don't have to try really hard to distribute it to you. If they claim that they could not find you after two years, they get to keep the money. In my view, they don't try hard enough, and you should take the time to read the section "Why Your Lawyer Won't Help You Get This Money," which explains my personal experience with this, to understand why you cannot simply trust your lawyer or personal manager to do this task.

Naturally, you don't have to sign up with and monitor all of these agencies. Just the ones that cover the regions where you think or know your music is getting action. See the sidebar "NRO Territories" for a list.

NRO Territories: Countries That Are a Party to the Rome Convention

Argentina
Australia
Austria
Barbados
Belgium
Bolivia
Brazil
Bulgaria
Burkina Faso
Canada
Chile
Colombia
Congo
Costa Rica
Czech Republic
Denmark
Dominican Republic
Ecuador
El Salvador
Fiji
Finland
France
Germany
Great Britain and N. Ireland
Greece
Greenland
Guatemala
Honduras
Hungary
Iceland
Italy
Jamaica
Japan
Lesotho
Luxembourg
Mexico
Moldova
Monaco
Netherlands
Niger
Nigeria
Norway
Panama
Paraguay
Peru
Philippines
Republic of Ireland
Slovak Republic
Spain
Sweden
Switzerland
United Kingdom
Uruguay

Why Your Lawyer Won't Help You Get This Money

Actual reader question: "But I have an attorney and a business manager. Shouldn't I let the guy making 5%–20% worry about this NRO stuff?"

I'm going to tell you a very eye-opening story about having your manager or lawyer monitor this money for you. Some years back, a foreign informant discovered and disclosed to me that he had found over $1,000,000 in NRO money that was earmarked for US artists. The money was sitting in the account of an NRO for the Netherlands, SENA.

I contacted SENA, and sure enough, they told me that this money was all for US artists that they were having trouble locating. Artists like Metallica, Ricky Martin, John Mayer, Michael Jackson, Paul McCartney, Arrested Development, and Sting (Sting is a U.S. artist even though he is British, because he signed to a U.S. label)—you know, hard-to-find artists who have been hiding in the shadows. All these artists had to do was fill out the "artist in residency" forms and SENA applications and they could get paid.

I received a list of more than 100 artists who were owed money, and through my network of clients, readers, and lawyers, sent out messages to everyone, explaining that they were entitled to this cash, but had to claim it within the next 60 days.[1]

Some people responded quickly and were amazingly thankful. Some gave back a few bucks as a donation to artists' rights and to show their appreciation. But, oddly enough, some of the larger acts, who were still in the mainstream and making big bucks, were not happy about me finding this new money. Ricky Martin was owed $90,000 for "La Vida Loca." I told Desmond Child, the song's producer,

---

1. This money had been sitting there for almost two years, and was about to expire in the next two months. What does "expire" mean? By the laws that establish and govern NROs, if, after two years, the agency cannot find the rightful author for the money it collects, then the money goes into a "Black Box." (This box is metaphorical. There is no actual box, only an escrow account in a foreign bank.) The money gets transferred there and then gets divided up among all the NROs and their agents. What a sweet deal for an NRO. They get rewarded for their laziness.

directly about this cash at a conference in LA. Since he is an author of the sound recording some of this money was his. He thanked me and apparently did nothing because his share of the SENA money was never claimed.

Sting and Yoko Ono (as trustee for the John Lennon estate) used the same financial services person. Lennon was owed $12,000; Sting was owed $7,500. Found money for both, yet, when I asked for thank-you letters that I could post on my site so that other artists would know that this SENA money was for real and not some "we can find you lost royalties" scam (of which there are several). I was told through their accountant, with whom I was dealing, that both artists refused. Many lawyers who represented medium- and large-name artists never even bothered to claim their cash either. WTF?

It took me a little while to figure it out. Well, I didn't actually figure it out at all. I was called in for a sit-down with some industry lawyers, who basically scolded me for exposing the very existence of this money and embarrassing them in the process.

You see, many artists use a lawyer who works on a 5% commission to handle their business affairs. So, from the lawyer's point of view, he needs to justify his time against his billing rate of between $350 and $600 per hour. In other words, if he is working on a percentage, the time he spends servicing the client should net to the billing rate.

Now, SENA, like all NROs, doesn't make it easy to get this money the first time out; you have to fill out about several long forms and, if you're the artist's lawyer, show proof that you're the legal agent to collect this money on behalf of your artist. All this takes several hours. In many cases the money owed to these known artists was not more than $15,000. Five percent of $15K is $750—less than two hours at most top attorneys' billing rates. From a cost/benefit point of view, this was a loser; plus, the lawyer would have to disclose to their very busy, temperamental, and often financially un-savvy client that they goofed and had missed collecting thousands for the past two years. All things considered, it was easier to let it slip away into the Black Box. Who making over a million a year will miss $15,000?

Out of $1,060,000 dollars that was on the table, less than $250,000 of it found its way into the pockets of the US artists it was owed to. The rest slipped into European oblivion. I have not undertaken this task since. Moral: Don't let your lawyer set this up. Do it yourself. Learn about how this money works. If you don't want the money, like Desmond and Ricky, and you're too rich to care, donate it. I'm sure someone else could use it.

Public Performance of a Song

As you may have figured out by now, if you're a songwriter, simply joining the US Performing Rights Organizations (PROs) ASCAP, BMI, or SESAC is not really enough. It's true that each of these US PROs has tentacles that reach overseas and agreements to take aggregated monies from foreign PROs. It's also true that all that means is that this money will go into the meat grinder of ASCAP and BMI's pooling system, and in the case of SESAC, towards their bonus system. In all three cases these systems, according to many reports, seem to favor the bigger writers and publishers. How can you circumvent this? Simple: There is a PRO for every country in the free world; just join every single one of them.

The Procedure

Some have said that this is not possible to do. But they are mistaken. The process is far easier if you have yet to join a US PRO. If you're already signed to one first, you'll have to do something socially unacceptable: you'll have to carve out foreign rights with them. That is a negotiation that some artists would rather not bother with. If you're a renowned songwriter you'll have a bit more ammunition, especially if you're doing this around contract renewal time, and the veiled threat is that you'll jump to your PRO's competitor if they don't come to a compromise with you.

Some PRO reps will tell you that you can only belong to one PRO at a time, but they are referring to *US* PROs, not a combination of foreign and US PROs. It's true you can only belong to one US PRO at a time (and there is a workaround for that, too), but there is no law preventing you from parsing out your foreign rights. Don't let anyone tell you otherwise. Policy is not law. So, when a rep for a PRO says, "You can only belong to one," they are essentially trying to confuse you so they can preserve control over the distribution of over $5 billion a year worldwide.

But you can take back some control over your money by giving them an "exemption letter" that states what territories you want carved out. They won't respond with a smile. Most people never ask, because they do not know that it's possible.

If you have not yet signed with a US PRO, then I recommend that you put it off until you *first* sign with all the foreign PROs that you plan to monitor yourself. Then, when you sign with the US PRO of your choice, present them with the Exemption Letter. You'll get almost no flak (because no PRO would try to dissuade you from breaking a preexisting contract with another PRO).

In other words, when you first sign with a US PRO (or if you change PROs) you'll instruct them *not* to collect on your behalf from their foreign counterparts in specific territories. They'll hem and haw and tell you that is a big mistake, and if you have hits, they could possibly be right: the work involved in squeezing money out of thousands of radio spins, TV airs, and live venues is too daunting if you have international hits. But the savings can be well worth it. You'll see when you read the benefits section on the next page.

But for most of you reading this, you probably don't have any big hits; in fact, you're probably pretty peeved that you've heard your songs on the radio, TV, etc., and yet your PRO is telling you that it didn't show up on their surveys (see page 134 for why they probably never will, either).

If you have already signed up, then you'll have to wait until your contract is up (most PRO deals last a year). Then negotiate the carving out of these territories upon resigning. After you've freed these rights, then you can assign them to various other agencies and develop direct relationships with them.

Now, after pissing off your PRO, what are some of the benefits of reassignment?

1. You Get Your Overseas Money About Three Years Earlier. With ASCAP, BMI and SESAC, foreign money has to go through a long series of accounting periods before it even gets to your pool (see page 105 if you don't know what I mean by "pool") and long before it gets to your pocket, if ever. At each stage is a deduction and a full accounting period before it's passed on to the next link in the distribution process. An accounting period for all US PROs, by contract, is six months. So a key benefit of direct licensing is getting your money faster.

However, there is a caveat. The first time, it takes about two to three years for all the PROs to get in sync with each other after you've filed all this new paperwork. Be patient with the process. After it's all connected, the above will apply.

2. You Get More Money Because There Are Less Admin Fees. Each link in the collection/distribution chain charges an admin fee of between 10% and 15%. So, if you are an ASCAP member and are owed $1,000 from SOCAN, SOCAN takes a 10% fee, leaving $900. They wait till the end of each accounting period (six months), and then pass it on to ASCAP, which then takes another 15% (roughly), leaving you with only $765, which they pay you in another six months. If you have a direct deal you get all $900 about six months earlier, and save that extra vig. (ASCAP does not charge a flat percentage. These numbers are merely to illustrate the example.) The actual amount of the fees are based on complex accounting procedures.

3. Bigger Splits, Yo. In the US the 50/50 split of public performance money between publisher and composer is sacrosanct. But around the world things are different; composers in many cases get 66% and the publishers only 33%. (To see why, keep reading.) Direct licensing means a bigger cut for you. This is not true of every country.

4. Pension Qualifications. Unlike the US, in some European countries if you've massed enough plays, you're eligible for a pension. This is particularly true for SACEM, the performing rights organization of France. The French (and indeed several European countries) tend to nurture their artists, and feel that a pension is the least they can do for the creation of a great piece of art. In the US this philosophy is given lip service by politicians, but is considered laughably socialistic by our standards.

So . . . you can see why your US PRO would try to dissuade you from carving out European rights. If you did, they could not make money floating your cash, or working the exchange rates or the extra admin fees. Money traveling through several agencies over two years also makes it harder to audit them. Think this is too nickel-and-dime to pay an entire department over $1,000,000 a year to do nothing but monitor foreign exchange rates and overseas collections? *That's* what it's worth to *them*. The real question is, what is it worth to *you*?

Ask your PRO rep if she thinks parsing out your foreign collection rights is a good idea and listen carefully to the reasons as to why it's not. She'll be hard-pressed to make a good argument other than that it's a lot of work for you and "we" do all that already for you. Yep, they do—for a rate of about 25%, and many months of float.

See the Appendix for a complete list of foreign PROs.

What Are the Numbers: How Many Acts per Year Do the Major Labels Sign and Release?

When I saw this question, I was pleased. "Someone is looking at the long odds," I thought. When you go to Vegas, the odds to each game are readily available: roulette, 33:1; blackjack, 1.5:1 (if played optimally); craps, anywhere from 2:1 to 9:1. But what about the chances of getting signed and having a successful career recording albums?

Sure, there a lot of factors, like if you've got any talent, if you've got cash to invest, if you've got relatives that can kick open a door or two—but what about the raw odds? (The "Vegas odds," as they are called.) I did some research and was intrigued to find that there are no published stats on this. So I created some. Here, perhaps for the first time, are the Vegas odds of record deals and your chances of success with them.

Ready?

Each year approximately 43,000 demos are sent to the 35 labels that I would consider to be "major," and only 1,000 new acts are signed to the four major US record distributors or their affiliates to deals of various sizes and types. It's not an even split. Universal, with all its combined majors, signs about 800 new acts a year. Warner, with all its combined debt, signs about 80. Sony/BMG, with all its international muscle and lateral integration, signs about 300, and EMI when healthy signs about 150 acts a year, and when it seesaws the other way, it cuts back to between 10 and zero. Mind you, these can be anything from demo deals to complete, multi-album 360 Deals.

Don't worship these numbers. They fluctuate depending on several factors, like the past year's success, surplus budget, and if anybody is still working in the A&R department after the 2006–2009 house cleaning. But for the sake of this discussion, we can say with confidence that 1,000 seems to be a good round number. And by the way, that number has not changed much since 2001, when many feel that artist development started a progressive downhill slide. The reality is that the budget for each has been slashed, but the number of acts signed themselves has only dipped a bit. And you'll see why in a second.

So, the raw odds of even getting signed if you submit your demo to a major label are about 43:1. Just a little bit worse than playing 00 on the roulette wheel. Tough, but not the "million to one" shot often hyperbolized. Now . . .

Of these 1,000 major label signings it used to be that half were released to the public. Since 2008, however, this number has been reduced to about 300, or about 3:1. Of the 300 released, 50%, or 150, will sell enough records to justify a second advance to record a second album. So your odds of a new act recording a second album on a major are about 6:1 after you beat the 43:1 odds of getting signed.

Of that 150, about 75 will make a third album. Of the 75 that make a third album, only about 50 will make a fourth album on the same major label, or have their contract "upstreamed" to a parent label. This is usually the break-even point for the artist. In other words, to get to the break-even point, even after getting signed to that dream deal, you're still facing odds of about 24:1 of developing a multi-album career through the major label system. So far that brings the raw odds to about 1,000:1 to go from dream to reality.

The other 950 acts who didn't advance to their fourth album may go on to make records in the independent world or in self-released land, or they may continue to tour and sustain careers through merchandise sales or master

licensing. Many become soundtrack composers, producers, label owners, lawyers, etc. Some leave the business altogether.

Each year this process is repeated. Which means that 1,000 freshmen acts a year enter the artist development grinder, and four albums or about seven years later, 50 "graduates" will remain from that class, still working within the major label contracts they signed. In this way majors extend their stable of talent at a cost/benefit ratio of 20:1.

When major labels say that only 5% of the artists they sign "make money," this is the basic concept they are referring to. However, this is misleading. Almost any artist who has made it to the point of even a third album has grossed in the hundreds of thousands, probably millions, through publishing, merchandise, touring, and endorsements, and has satisfied their initial investors. So, in truth, the label itself has seen millions in revenue, even though they enjoy implying otherwise with their clever play on the words "make money."

In essence, even if most major label signings don't result in the creation of a superstar, the dropped acts still generate enough ancillary interest to create mini-empires with myriad revenue streams. These are the one-hit wonders who still tour and generate appeal off their hit from 10 years ago, or the songstresses like Suzanne Vega or the Indigo Girls who sell respectable numbers but are sort of off the mainstream radar these days, or the '90s hair bands doing a reunion tour that still sell out 5,000-seat venues. And remember—these are considered the "failures" by the high-bar major label standards. On the "winning" side of the formula you have groups like U2, the Rolling Stones, Madonna, and other superstars, who individually earn well into the hundreds of millions a year.

But there's more: The odds have an interesting dynamic if you survive the game a few years. Let's say you're signed to a Universal label. In year one you're competing with the other 799 freshmen plus the already existing 1,500 or so senior acts that have survived the elimination process from previous years. So you're competing with about 2,300 acts in year one, when you're recording your first album that you'll be delivering in year three.

Now, in year three, you're gearing up for your second album, you are competing with the same 1,500 catalog acts, the 800 new acts Universal signed the year after you were signed, and the 299 remaining acts from your class. So in year one you have 2,300 total competitors, but in year three you've got about 2,600.

For your third (or junior) release, it will be year five and now you've got the 800 acts signed that year, the 1,500 catalog acts, the remaining 300 from the class after you, and the 149 remaining in your class. So, about 2,750.

You can see where this is going. The longer you stay in the game, the larger the field becomes and the harder it is to get attention. It's like a reverse tournament: instead of players being eliminated at each level, new ones are added, with fresh resources and stamina. Just like Vegas, the longer you play, the harder it is to win.

Staying Indie

Think your chances of success are better without a big label? Think a 24:1 ratio once you get signed and get through the seven-year, four-album labyrinth is still bad enough that you're better off staying indie? Here's a statistic to chew on: In 2009 all labels of every size, including vanity labels that are artist-owned, released approximately 100,000 titles in the US. According to Nielsen SoundScan, just a little over 2,000 of them sold more than 5,000, which for an indie is often thought of as the break-even point for a CD album. So in the indie world the odds of breaking even are roughly 50:1.

These are far worse odds than the 24:1 odds on the majors—not even counting the fact that in the major label world you'll be getting advances and tour support as you "fail." So, if you're looking at the Vegas odds for your music career, a major label deal, sucky as it can be, is still the best bet in the house.

Of course, this is a crude interpretation of raw numbers. The fact is that if your music is not appropriate for a major label and you somehow get signed by them anyway, your odds will likely be far worse than 24:1, and you'll be more like the 2,500:1 fodder that gets dropped. If you're very talented and well-financed privately, your odds of making a decent living are better off by staying indie, in the short run. In the long run, however, to build a long-term infrastructure in your music, you will need some type of distribution partner. So, the odds are a must play even though they sort of suck. If you're going to step into the casino of the music business, there is no avoiding the fact that you're gambling. All you can do is look to place the best bets with the least amount of downside.

How Much Do the Majors/ Indies Budget for Studio Recordings?

It almost seems like the indie world and major label world live in two separate universes. In the major world the same things seems to cost about four times the money. An album that an indie recorded will cost about $35,000, and a major will spend $350,000, and yet they will sound identical and may even be recorded in the same studio with the same engineers. How come?

Two reasons: One is how much people will charge you to do the same job, and two is how much you pay yourself.

1. Studio rates change as you climb the ladder. The main reason prices go up so radically hinges around the economics of recording studios. Studios have three sets of rates: 1) "card rate," which is their advertised rate; 2) "professional rate," which is what they will actually settle on, usually about half the card rate; and 3) "favor rate," which is the very least amount for which they will book time. It is usually bumpable, meaning that if a higher-paying client calls for time, the favor-rate client will be bumped from the session. Favor rate is usually 50%

to 70% below card rate. Add to this the fact that many studios will do six-day weeks and 20-day months if you pay in cash or have a good report with them. Ironically, larger studios are in a better position to offer discounts than smaller ones, and so you can get a better value there even though you pay more.

2. You treat yourself better. No, you didn't take a self-esteem class or dump that lousy boyfriend/girlfriend. Major labels require that you pay yourself union-level wages for your performances in the studio. Members of a band and even the artist need to be paid union scale to perform on their own records. As the artist climbs the ladder of success, they must charge themselves double or triple scale for their time. If they ask a friend in another successful band to be a soloist on their record, the friend will get a higher fee as well. This money comes out of your recording fund.

So, in indie land you're signed to Mad Dog, get the bumpable studio rate, your buddy who just mixed a platinum record does you a favor for $35/hour *cash* and cuts the tracks, you work at night, and pay yourself zilch. Budget for album: about $5,000–$25,000.

Now Sony buys out Mad Dog's contract on you. The game changes for the better. You pay yourself a union rate, pay at least the pro rate for the same studios you used to piss in for free, pay a producer $35K for showing up and picking his nose, insurance costs, cartage, an instrument tech, etc. Album budget: $150,000.

The Sony deal blows up. You're a fat-ass superstar. National tour, five-star hotels. Kid Rock thinks you're a god. You need Studio A at Right Track available to you 24/7 for three months, no interruptions, with the private entrance and entourage/game room. No more tuna fish sandwiches for lunch. You're ordering in from top-notch places, have chefs making you your favorite snack at 3 a.m., have a top-notch producer who takes 30% of the budget as his fee. Album budget: $500,000. Ain't life grand?

Major Label Recording Budgets

As you can see, the cost of doing business more than doubles once a plateau of success is established, mainly for two reasons: 1) Vendors are less likely to discount their rates; and 2) the artists pay themselves more and treat themselves to better accommodations.

	New Artist	Mid-level Artist (or one that is in demand)
Basic Tracks		
Three weeks at large studio ($1,500 per day "card rate"), discounted[8]	$9,000	$22,500
Engineer ($400–$750 per day)	Included in studio fees	$13,500
Media		
Tape (2-inch 24-track)—20 reels @ $150 per reel (old school) or Pro Tools rig rental by the day—	—	$3,000
three 100 GB hard disk sidecars ($250 each)	$750	—
Overdubs		
Union scale musicians' fees for the backup band—$350 per player per day (four players)[9]	$29,400	$58,800 (double scale)
Smaller studio ($1,000 per day) for four weeks, discounted	—	$30,800
Smaller studio ($500 per day) for four weeks, discounted	10,000	—
Union scale musicians' fees for the band—$350 per player per day (two players)	$14,000	$28,000 (double scale)
Side players/guest soloists	$3,000	$10,000
Engineer ($400–$1,100 per day)	$8,000	$30,800
Mixing		
Mix studio—$2,500 per day (15–36 days)	$37,500	$90,000
Hard drive rentals	$600	$600
Digital backup/storage	$200	$500

Mix engineer ($1,000–$1,500 per day)	$15,000	$54,000
Single mix (for promotion)	$5,000 (1 single)	$50,000 (2 singles @ $25,000 each)
Producer's fee	$20,000	$110,000
Miscellaneous Cartage	(artist pays for own)	$10,000
Lodging	Stay with a friend	$30,000
Strings/sticks/skins, etc.	$1,000	$2,500
Mastering	$1,500	$10,000
Total	**$154,950**	**$555,000**

How Much Do the Majors/Indies Budget for Tour Support?

Tours last from four to six weeks for baby acts and six to 12 weeks for larger national acts. International acts know no real time limits. They go where they want when they want, and budget is a thing they make up based on higher math versus just what they can afford.

Major labels generally give a new act $75,000 in what they call "Deficit Tour Support." Put simply, that means you pay for it and they will reimburse you for up to $75K (usually 50% recoupable). It is enough? Let's see.

On a scale of 1 to 10, with 1 being "I'm still looking for a break while I tour the local dives within a 50-mile radius of where we rehearse," and 10 being "we're trying to decide what Lear jet to rent because using commercial flights to get from our gig in New York to Paris in one night is stressing us out," I'm guessing that, if you're currently on a decent-size label, and have your first song on in FM rotation, you're hovering somewhere around a 6, on my scale. The following advice is rounded for this zone, between a 5 and an 8. For advice below the 5 zone, consult the earlier chapters. For advice above the 8 zone, call me.

Now, although I was a front-end sound mixer for several medium-size national acts during my tenure as an engineer, my knowledge of tour financing is anecdotal. So, I asked some colleagues to contribute to this section. What follows is an assimilation of their experience.

Mini Tours

Three-week runs where you're tagging onto one leg of an existing national act that is touring the entire US for six months.

At this level you will certainly have to "buy" your way onto a decent tour. Back in the '60s and '70s, an opening act slot was generally given as a gift by a major act to a friend who was a local act on his way up. They changed opening acts with each city. No more. Tours have become highly commercialized on the internal side. In other words, promoters, and bands themselves, have learned that ticket sales are only one form of revenue that a tour earns. You can charge money to each vendor who wants to service your fans. That includes the opening slot.

I often get asked by new acts how they can get on a tour. The answer is simple: Get the money for the "buy-on." This is money paid to a tour-packaging agent, who then spreads it around to various persons who ultimately get you that opening slot. It's not like payola, which is covert and sneaky and a fraud. This is a legitimate fee paid to cover overhead and commissions for legitimate sales work. Support acts on an established package tour (such as Warped) or with an established arena act (such as Van Halen, Mötley Crüe, Dave Matthews, U2, etc.) will play to 15,000 to 40,000+ people per night—versus the club dates with the 300 to 1,000 people that the act could draw on their own. Bands and packages capable of playing such large venues are a very small minority of the industry as a whole— and they bargain accordingly! They also have many suitors. More struggling acts than headliners—always.

To do something like the five-day Warped Tour or carry a

one-week leg of a national act—a mini tour, in other words—a band would need about $80K. It would break down like this:

➜ $50,000 – Buy-on fee.
➜ $8,000 – Crew salaries: driver, merch master at arms (often a girlfriend), personal roadie/drum tech/guitar tech (one manager, I also suggest a good mid-level tour manager; which may be a tick more if there are headline gigs along the tour)
➜ $5,000 – Transportation (in a van you already own)
➜ $10,000 – Lodging (don't expect more than the Days Inn at this level)
➜ $7,000 – Miscellaneous (repairs to gear, incidentals, per diem [$20/day])

If you're asking yourself where the first $50K goes, don't ask. It will just make you mad to find out. It's a commission paid to several people, but mainly it is a pay to play fee. You want exposure? This tour will give it to you. Exposure is not cheap. It's a form of advertising. You wouldn't expect a network to air your commercial during the Super Bowl for free, would you? No. Supermarkets charge food distributors to put products on certain shelves, or on the corner of aisles to get better noticed by shoppers. Grocery stores get marketing money from vendors whose products are displayed in their weekly ads. You think candy is *always* on the bottom shelf because there is no room at the top? No; it's because children can reach it there. You want music fans to sample *your* candy? You have to put it where it can be reached. A national tour is prime shelf space. Nothing more. "The Tour" will provide millions in advertising/press that would otherwise have been unavailable via purchasers, sponsors, and associated publicists, including a dedicated tour publicist.

However, it's not just a gatekeeper fee. Part of what you're paying for is to ensure that you're getting solid potential for "conversion." That means new people who have not heard of you but will convert and become a fan after hearing you. The packaging agent's job is to get you placed where it will do the most good. There's no point in putting you on a rap tour if you're a skinhead act.

I know the numbers and the debt seem quite daunting, but one has to balance this with the fact that an $80K-plus investment will probably yield millions of dollars in exposure in national print, radio interviews, increased airplay, and playing in front of 250,000+ people who don't necessarily know your music and wouldn't otherwise. Remember, if it was money poorly spent, why would it be done so often? To get some perspective on this, take a look at *Pollstar*'s box office reports. They show where bands play in their "natural" position in the world versus where they can play with a buy-on. And all this is designed to get you to the next level.

Mid-Level Tours

A more established act (one with perhaps a gold single/album) would generally budget about double the mini tour: between $120,000 and $150,000. Are they paying themselves more? No, not really. Per diems notch up a bit to about $30 a day. So this is negligible.

A lot of the new money is eaten up by THE BUS. Yes, the big bus you always see parked out front with the cool psychedelic designs. That giant costs about $750 to $1,500 a day plus enough fuel to fly a B-52 to France, on a minimum 30-day contract, plus the driver's union-mandated lodgings. You get to sleep on the bus.

Other new expenses are costumes, sets, lighting/effects, the production and logistics of merchandise to be sold, and more crew: your own mixer and monitor person, security, and a tour manager to coordinate every aspect of the tour and interact with all the production staff, other acts, your agent, manager, girlfriends/boyfriends, groupies, and stalkers, and especially to make sure you get on the bus and on to the next gig on time in one piece.

When it comes to the buy-on, do you think you get a break now that you've pierced the bubble with a hit? Nope. You still pay, and it might even go up quite a bit. In the case of a newer platinum-selling artist going on an arena band tour with Mötley Crüe or Aerosmith, the buy-on could be as high as $250K. (In a rare event, it could be zero if they have the same management or the national act wants to try to poach fans from the sophomore act.) This type of attitude makes the Sunset Strip club owners who mandate that you buy $200 worth of tickets to your own show seem benevolent.

Now keep in mind that older acts don't do five- to six-night weeks, preferring at most three or four dates per week. This means you pay more but get fewer chances to perform and sell merch. So, you'll try to fill in dates with smaller clubs or events that follow the headliner's tour route, hoping to score a $5,000–25,000 gig here and there to defray some fixed costs like crew and bus rental. Here the smart manager will occasionally try to acquire sponsorship opportunities. Perhaps energy drink "Mule Piss" will be provided for your tour bus if you appear in their print ads and allow them to wrap their billboard around your bus. Maybe Guitar Center will provide your techs with something similar.

In addition there will be the supporting marketing budget to promote and market the tour/act itself. This is a separate line item. See the following table for a sample marketing budget.

Sample Tour Budget for a Baby Band

Salaries	Per Week	# of Weeks	Total
Tour Mgr.	$1,400.00	16	$22,400.00
Tour Asst./Roadie	400.00	16	6,400.00
Drum Tech	400.00	16	6,400.00
Guitar Techs	400.00	16	6,400.00
Payroll Taxes			7,336.00
Total Salaries			**$48,936.00**

Per Diems		Daily Rate	# of Days	Total
Band	(4)	$25.00	120	($12.000.00)
Tour Mgr.	(1)	30.00	120	3,600.00
Crew	(3)	25.00	120	9,000.00
Total Per Diems				**$24,600.00**

Bus Expense	Rate/Wk.	# of Weeks	Total
Bus Lease	$3,150.00	16	$50,400.00
Trailer	315.00	16	5,040.00
Driver	1,470.00	16	23,520.00
Overdrives	210.00	16	3,360.00
Rep. & Maint.	150.00	16	2,400.00
Total Bus Lease			**$84,720.00**

Fuel	Total Miles	Cost/Mile	Total
Fuel for Bus	28,000	$0.38	$10,640.00
Total Bus Expense			**$10,640.00**

Lodging	Cost/Night	# of Nights	Total
Dayrooms (band and crew) (2)	$75 per rm.	60	$9,000.00
Driver Room (1)	$75 per rm.	120	$9,000.00
Total Lodging			**$18,000.00**

Tour Insurance	Per Show	# of Shows	Total
General Liab., Auto, Equip. Annual	$100.00	100	$10,000.00
Total Tour Insurance			**$10,000.00**

Other	Total
Booking Agent	—
Manager Commission	—
Business Manager	—
Production Expenses	—
Phones/Faxes	$600.00
Tourbooks	600.00
Misc. Supplies/Gaffe Tape/Strings/Sticks	1,200.00
Total Other	**$2,400.00**

Net Tour Support Required	199,296.00

Marketing for the Road

Just as you would hire a street team to market your album when it's released, you would also spend time and money to make sure your fans, old and new, are aware that you're coming to town. Below is how much it typically costs to do that for a mid-level act with their first hit under their belts and a second album due out in a few months. This act is wisely synchronizing their tour with the album's release to gain maximum leverage and piggyback off the money the label is spending on album promotion. If done correctly and with a little luck they can make their $60,000 investment yield the results of a $250,000 marketing effort. Remember: the promoter in *each market* will be buying tens of thousands of dollars in ads to promote this show, leaning on local radio to help build excitement (playing the act's songs) to sell tickets, and the label will be piggybacking on all this with contests, magazine ads, press articles, talk show performances—maybe even *Saturday Night Live*!

Month	Category	Description	Cost
May **Month 1**	CEG	Set up marketing/team admin./tool prod. & dist.	$6,500
	New Media	Develop myspace/pv.com/peer sites and URL/**4-month plan**	$3,500
	Production/Design	Tools/stickers, postcards, etc.	$10,000
June **Month 2**	CEG	Set up marketing/mainstream online setup	$6,500
	New Media	Develop myspace/pv.com/peer sites and URL	$3,500
	Lifestyle Marketing	Street & retail awareness/**3-month plan**	$2,500
July **Month 3**	CEG	Set up marketing/mainstream online setup	$6,500
	New Media	Third-party seeding and online press	$3,500
	Lifestyle Marketing	Add tour coverage and focus markets	
			$2,500
August **Month 4**	**Band begins US tour/Label to begin marketing TBD**		
	CEG	Set up marketing/mainstream online setup/retail support	$6,500
	New Media	Third-party seeding and online press	$3,500
	Lifestyle Marketing	Street & retail awareness & tour coverage	$3,500
August	**ALBUM RELEASE**		
Total			**$58,500**

Thanks to Chuck Griffiths for his help with this section.

What Is "Payola"?
Why Is It Important?
Will It Ever Stop?

If you're now a semi-pro or pro artist, you're savvy enough to approach this subject maturely and with more sophistication than the average newbie who thinks payola is a conspiracy to keep him from getting his songs on the air, which he knows are far better than the "crap out there."

Sound familiar? Read on.

A Bit of History

In 1960, Alan Freed, a famous radio DJ, was indicted for accepting $2,500 for playing a song many times on his radio show, *Rock N Roll Dance Party*. Alan claimed the money was a token of gratitude from the label and did not affect his choice of what he played on his famous radio show. He was obviously lying. He paid a small fine and was back on the air in no time. But Freed's indictment clearly defined the practice of *covertly* accepting money to influence what was played on the public airwaves as "bribery." Newspapers used the word "payola," which was a contraction of the words "pay" and "Victrola" (a popular antique LP record player made by RCA in the 1940s–1960s).

Both radio stations and record companies claimed that the practice was necessary. Labels needed to promote their goods and had the right to hire salesmen, and radio stations needed a filter to help assess the public's opinion and weed out the junk. They argued that to have a DJ listen to every new recording would be far too labor-intensive and costly.

All of these defenses, accurate as they were, fell on deaf ears, and soon a new law made payola a misdemeanor, with a stiff penalty of up to $10,000 and one year in prison. The game got serious, but that did not stop the practice in any way. In fact, like most necessities that are made illegal for political reasons, it only made the practice more expensive.

Payola fees soared to $300,000 per song, hitting a speed

bump in the mid-1970s when a second set of indictments pushed many DJs out of their booths and into permanent retirement. DAs, who have always had a thing for bagging the music biz, claimed that payola was perpetrating fraud on the public, since radio was making use of the "publicly owned" airwaves. They connected payola to the RICO Act, and brought in stiffer fines and long potential prison terms. Record companies again cried foul, claiming that payola was no different from political lobbying or paying a supermarket for better product placement—such as at eye level on a more desirable aisle—which has been proven to increase sales. DAs continued to argue against both record companies and radio stations for years without success, mainly because it was hard to make a solid case when you could not prove that a fee was paid for a *specific* song. Also, to the average juror, who just wanted to hear good music on the radio, the entire matter sounded political.

So the practice of payola raged on, becoming more sophisticated in the 1980s. People specializing in the service went from greasy bagmen with many vowels in their names to "independent promoters." Record companies hired these promoters to pimp recordings to the program directors of major radio stations. A certain elite group of independent promoters emerged called "The Network." Each member of the Network had his own US territory. If a record company wanted a single played nationally, it had to hire the entire Network. The Network or one of its subcontractors would then get a song on the air by any means necessary—offering hookers, cars, cash, you name it.

In 2001, when Clear Channel bought most of the radio stations in the US, a major change took place in the payola industry. Instead of money given for a slot in a playlist, Clear Channel paid for "market research." Promoters now wore ties and used "market analysis" software to show a station's program director that what they were doing was anything but "pay for play"—their choice reflected the public's desires, and the fees were not for the hype, but for the research. These promoters are now called "radio consultants."

What Alan Freed began by accepting a $2,500 "present" has grown into a multimillion-dollar institution. Some estimates claim that before the downsizing of the music industry began in 2007, the Big Four major labels spent about $40 million on payola. Despite a recent set of indictments by now disgraced New York attorney general Eliot Spitzer, the practice continues and always will, regardless of whether we call it a bribe or "market research."

Is All This Worth It to the Label/Artists?

The airwaves are still the most effective way for labels to advertise their product—the artist. And getting a song in constant rotation brings with it the hope that by pure repetition over the air, people will "learn to like the record," generating a sale. There is plenty of marketing data to confirm that this works, but here is a bit of solace for you purists out there. Although record companies tend to be very secretive about which promotion scams work and which ones don't, I believe in the Abe Lincoln philosophy, which goes (and I'm paraphrasing), "You can make most of the people buy a crappy record some of the time, and you can make some of the people buy a crappy record most of the time, but you can't make most of the people buy a crappy record most of the time."

Basically, in the long run, you can't make enough people buy a record they hate, no matter how much money you throw at it. Although it seems that major labels sure do try.

Net Hype: The Newest Payola

Now that the Internet is the hip new way to promote singles, independent promoters have become very clever—hiring scores of college students to "assist with promotion" by going into chat rooms and hyping new artists. They're not the only ones doing this. Unsigned artists commonly use bulk e-mail incentives to get people to go to an online record company and "vote" or click on their single in hopes of inflating their apparent appeal. They know that A&R people watch these statistics to see who is getting attention. It seems to work. In the past two years, several new artists were "discovered" this way by major labels.

So Is It a Conspiracy After All?

Not really. It's business. Garage bands send their stuff to radio stations, but it gets rejected. In their minds they think that payola is holding them back from getting their (better) songs on the air. But this frame of mind is like someone who makes coffee at a diner wanting to open up their own Starbucks, and then blaming "corporate corruption" when they are turned down by Starbucks for an $8 million loan and franchise license. They begin to think that you can only open a Starbucks by paying people off or having an uncle at the company. This person doesn't care that they only made coffee in a Greek diner for a year or two. Experience is for squares, right?

The above situation might seem ridiculous, but this is how mainstream radio views new artists who have no label backing or a national platform. Why should we "lend" you the airtime when you don't have the following? The real reason the coffee maker can't get a franchise (and thus, in our analogy, can't "compete with the major labels") is that he has not proven, through sales statistics, that he knows anything about coffee distribution or marketing campaigns. But Starbucks knows for a fact that without this knowledge, giving him a multimillion-dollar opportunity is probably a waste of their resources.

Giving an unknown act a very valuable airplay slot when they have no method of exploiting it is unfair to *everyone*, mainstream radio stations believe. It's unfair to the local act, who will not be able to leverage the exposure into meaningful sales, and it's unfair to the national act that should have gotten that opportunity but was pushed aside because of some weird type of radio affirmative action.[2]

But rather than learn more about boring things like how a P&L sheet works,[3] which takes time and money, the unknown artist takes what appears to be a more socially acceptable path: he complains about what he does know about: *corporate corruption*, greed, and nasty capitalists who import coffee from third-world nations. He authors more rhetoric, which he can read and chat about with his "friends" on Facebook. The cancer grows in the psyche of the disgruntled musician/coffee maker: It must be corruption keeping him from his dream, because if there were any other possible reasons, he would know about them, because after all, he works in the coffee business every day—serving coffee.

Who Should I Hire to Pimp My Track?

This is a far trickier question to answer. There are many indie promoters out there. The best thing to do is get a personal recommendation. There are too many sleazy tricks employed by independent promoters for you to "catch" them in a lie.

One common one, used by a great majority, is to name drop and claim they worked on a campaign for a particular song, when in fact they were merely one of many assistants who worked for a subcontractor, and not the company that was hired directly. Fact: Very few indie promoters actually push major acts to radio, yet thousands of promoters will claim a connection to national acts.

If the company you're considering claims this, here's what you can do: Call the artist's management, be ultra polite and say that you are checking references, and ask if it's true that so-and-so was the promoter for a particular region. (Remember that

---

2. Radio Affirmative Action: In 2007, as part of the Clear Channel payola settlement of the 2005 suit brought by then attorney general Eliot Spitzer, the company was required to give 1,200 hours of airtime to unsigned acts. They did. It produced no significant effect on music sales or careers—even for the acts who received the airtime.

3. "P&L": Profit and Loss. A balance sheet that describes if a situation is profitable. Used in every business venture, including the music industry.

terrestrial radio promotion is a *regional* business.) You can't ask the local stations, as they will likely not want you or anyone to know who their promoter is.

My office offers recommendations on this subject. We keep a database of complaints about indie promoters. If the person you're inquiring about is not in our database, he's probably okay. Don't just call us on a whim, however; there are fees for this service. For more on this subject, turn to the section on Scamsters, page 51.

Do I Need a Written Business Plan? How Do I Do It?

Yes. You do. I know; this sucks. "Why do I have to write this down—isn't it obvious how we intend to make money?" Well, no. In fact, in the past few years even major labels have had to justify their existence to their stockholders with written business plans—each year. Why? Because even they do not know exactly how music will be monetized over the next two decades.

Now, if they don't know for sure, it's very likely that Uncle Bob or Aunt Sue, whom you want to cut you a check, is going to want to know that you've really thought this music thing out before they invest in you.

Never before has the music space been as tricky to navigate as right now. As we're learning, all this new technology is a double-edged sword. It offers a lot of great opportunities with one hand while taking away or obsoletizing traditional ones with the other. It's forcing us to gamble or speculate with new techniques.

A business plan is really a learning tool. It masquerades as an advertisement that you know what you're doing. But sophisticated investors know that the creation of a plan does more than just prove that you know which end is up. An old saying goes that learning is finding out things you already know. Writing a business plan brings with it a magical transformation, a bonding between you and the data that could not exist by just "knowing" about it. The act of writing (or typing) brings with it a transformational process that is spiritual. When completed you'll feel more powerful, talk with greater authority, and be able to look people in the eye with a stronger conviction than those who are just sitting there passively with their hand out.

When potential investors or labels ask you what your penetration is in a given field, you'll know that they are not merely curious about how many fans you've boned on the road, but rather how many fans you created in a 50-square-mile region. How many CDs or downloads can you verify, and on what basis can you attest with a high degree of confidence that you can scale this number up to 100 fans if they loan you the cash.

Could you leave all this to your business manager? Sure, if you've got one. But in my experience, friends and family investors want to hear it from your mouth. They want to know that you're taking a scientific approach to your career, rather than just one based on social equity, hanging out, and writing great music.

How to Do It and What to Spend

There is a right way and wrong way to do a business plan. First, let's define exactly what we mean. A true business plan is about 40 pages long, and has a lot of stuff that nobody reads but that needs to be in there for legal purposes. If you're raising $1 million for a startup venture you need all of this, and there is only one right way to do it: hire a company that specializes in this service. It will cost about $10,000–$30,000 to write this plan.

The good news is that if you're starting a musical group you don't need to raise anywhere near that amount of money or have that elaborate a business plan. Full-length business plans come with what is called an "Executive

Summary." This is a five- to seven-page briefing. This is what most investors actually read, saving the other 30 or so pages of legal crap for their financial managers and lawyers. If you're only trying to raise a few hundred thousand, you probably only need an Executive Summary, even though you'll be calling it a "business plan." It's OK to interchange these terms *as long as you know the actual difference*, so that if prompted you don't sound like a charlatan trying to pass off a summary as a full-on plan.

Most people in the indie music scene use the term "business plan" when they really mean "Executive Summary." But you should know the difference when talking to actual prospects, and if they require additional information, be ready to give it to them.

But in nine out of 10 situations where friends and family raised money for a musical group, it was done with a short, five-page "business plan." This can be put together relatively cheaply. Many services will do it for about $5,000. At one time the Moses Avalon Company was charging that amount, but we've now done so many of them that the price has dropped to $1,500. That's the best price out there that I'm aware of. If you're going to shop this, make sure, however, that whoever is doing it cheaper is giving you the following:

➔ Complete bios of all players involved
➔ Mission statement(s)
➔ References

And most important . . .

➔ Five-year projection P&Ls done by a professional accountant on an interactive spreadsheet.

This last part will be the clincher, and will probably put their price way above the $1,500 mark. I have a CPA as a business partner, so I can do this as a value-added service. I suppose this could sound self-serving and a bit crass—using my book to pimp my services, but I'm only doing this so you know what your financial alternatives are and how much of your hard-earned cash you should be thinking about spending. If someone is quoting you $3,000, you should want to know why so much; if they are quoting you $700, you should be wary and want to know why so little, and make sure you're getting everything you need to make the plan buzz.

Think even $1,500 is too much to spend? Okay, no problem. There are many books out there on how to write an effective business plan. Do I have a problem with you reading one or more and DIYing this? Not really. But consider the time it will take you to absorb the information and process it. Then consider the time it will take you to do all the work, and then remember that you only get one shot at this. Do you want to fly in an airplane that you just built— and it's your first one? So, my advice is not to skimp here. I put this answer in part 3 instead of part 2 because you're now in the zone where every step counts, and you're smart enough to know what the stakes are.

Business plans are a pain in the butt, but one needs to be done, and in my experience you'll be thankful you did it afterwards. It will separate you from the thousands of bands, groups, and artists out there who say they're serious but can't even tell you at what point in their seven-year plan they will break even. They have the "Dude, it's about the music, not the money" plan. In other words, the "no plan" plan.

PART 4

I Want Out of This Deal

Questions and Answers for Those Who Have Had Enough

Introduction: They Never Said It Would Be Easy, but They Did Say It Would Be Fun

If you've turned to this chapter first, then I'm guessing that you've been kicked around by the biz and are a bit disillusioned. It's not the lifestyle advertised in music videos. Deal memo promises seem like hollow intentions made by manipulative "hipsters."

If you've read up to this chapter, then I'm guessing that you've seen enough of the good parts of the dream to keep you invested in the future of music. I'm with you. This is a tough business, and it's easy to say "I quit" the first or fifth time somebody screws you. But the alternative is . . . you could be working a lot harder for a lot less at something that is uncreative. Keep repeating that every time you think you've had enough.

For those who need a coach right now to tell them why all

this is worth it, I present the following questions and answers. Here is the benevolent optimism that will keep you tuned in and in tune.

With Digital Technology, It Is Possible to Track Almost All Performances. So Why Are the Societies Not Collecting or Paying the Royalties Due Their Independent Artists?

See below.

Why Do the U.S.-Based PROs Persist in Their Archaic and Inaccurate Method of Monitoring?

You'd think with all the advanced technology available to these companies taking in over $1 billion a year each that they could find a way to track what others making a tenth of their revenue are already tracking. But no. Why not? You can hold your iPhone up to a restaurant speaker and it will tell you what song is playing in seconds. Why can't this tagging and music ID technology be applied to tracking music on the airwaves more accurately in order to pay the songwriters?

Got a drink handy? This will not be a quickie.

A Short History of Data Collection

To understand this problem we need to time travel back to the year 2000 and look at the brief history of metadata. Zzzzzzz. Don't worry—I can sum up this up pretty quickly.

Before there was any kind of electronic data collection, radio stations would send 3.5-inch floppy disks and handwritten logs to the three PROs (Performing Rights Organizations: ASCAP, BMI, and SESAC) by snail mail. Then BMI (Broadcast Music, Inc.) began allowing the uploading of metadata to a log-in program using an FTP server. This eliminated the US mail and got a track count to the PRO quicker. Meanwhile, ASCAP was still having listeners fill out surveys. It seemed like BMI writers started making more money than their ASCAP counterparts, simply because of the speed at which data was arriving. To compete, ASCAP invested tons of cash in its own system, which promised to be a quantum leap above BMI's Internet-based system. ASCAP made a valid argument that BMI's system put the broadcaster/client on their honor to report accurately. Considering that BMI is owned by broadcasters, this seemed to be a reasonable concern for ASCAP.

Enter MediaGuide in 2002. Created through a partnership between ASCAP and ConneXus Corporation, MediaGuide began monitoring more than 2,500 US radio stations in real time, 24/7, across all commercial and noncommercial formats. MediaGuide does not use metadata, which is bits of information encoded within a CD. Nor does it rely on each station to send in anything. It uses fingerprinting and watermarking technologies; an active system that requires zero cooperation from the broadcaster. MediaGuide merely listens and reports.

For songwriters, this was a big step forward. MediaGuide even allowed the songwriters themselves to log into their charts on the MediaGuide website to see just how many spins of their music were tracked. But there were problems with the system. Now broadcasters were trusting their licensing bills to a machine that was owned and controlled by the licensee, ASCAP—the people they owed the money to. It was like having a taxi driver tell you how much you owed after the ride, on a meter he built in his garage and without telling you how it worked so you couldn't audit it yourself.

Licensing fees went up, and naturally broadcasters began to question the validity of the MediaGuide machine. But they could not argue with its methodology. Automated "listening" was clearly the future. Yet how could they keep the system honest?

Eventually other technologies—some independent, like BDS, which uses a digital sampling analysis; and some not, like Tunesat (both used by SESAC)—crept into the picture. These employed a combination of various technologies, both passive (watermarking and fingerprinting) and active (metadata and tagging). Each has its advantages and disadvantages that I'd rather not get into here—they're mind-numbing, and you need a degree from MIT to understand them all. (If you're really curious, do an Internet search for "fingerprinting vs. watermarking.") The bottom line is that none of these technologies can be trusted on its own, and some require that the broadcasters cooperate with the system, which defeats the purpose of having an automated system in the first place. Why would broadcasters want to help with this process? They are the ones paying close to $1.7 billion a year in fees. They have no desire to validate that figure (or, god forbid, invalidate it if it turns out to be too low).

To balance the scales, all the PROs agreed to have an independent auditor vet the data. This auditor, Music Reports, Inc., is in Woodland Hills, California. It owns an immense database of information that indicates who wrote what song, and what the splits are between the writers and publishers for each song. The auditor's fee to vet the bills from the PROs would be paid by the broadcasters. This seemed fair. If the PROs were going to own the bean counter, the auditor should be under the thumb of the broadcaster.

The Problem

So now that you know the players, here's the challenge. In order to have a system that instantly identifies all forms of music (songs and instrumental compositions) with pinpoint accuracy when played on the radio and TV, and that then creates a list of exactly how many times each song/composition is played on what station, along with durations and types of use, you'd need to do several things:

1. Add a metadata tag to each audio recording. This part is easy, and is done as a matter of course on newer recordings anyway, but older ones do not have it. I'm sure you've noticed that if you buy a used CD that was mastered before 1990 and try to rip it into iTunes, you cannot find the metadata on the Internet to fill in the title and song info. That's because putting metadata on CDs was not in practice at the time. For the system to really work, all gaps in the catalogs would have to be filled in by the labels that owned the masters. One problem: Who will pay for all this metadata insertion? Labels don't get any of this PRO money, and they have not exactly been on the PROs' holiday card list in recent years. So why should they do it? To help the PROs collect more money? H'yeah.

Labels may decide to get this done now that they will soon be getting paid for public performances of song masters, just like compositions; plus, new 360 Deals entitle them to the artist's publishing. So they may be incentivized soon. But even if all the majors did this to *every* old recording, indies would not have the budget or the resources to get it done, which means that you would still have a system that seems to favor the rich and ignores vast genres of American music copyrights.

The other possibility is to not rely on the label's remastering, but to allow fingerprinting systems like MediaGuide to do all the work. However, this too is not gap free, as it requires each song to be loaded into its tracking system so MediaGuide can put a tracking number (like a virtual bar code) on each master. But since they have to prioritize which ones go first, you can imagine who gets priority. Critics of this system argue that board members would cherry-pick who gets priority, and indeed already have done that. In ASCAP's case, some argue that their board is controlled by those who profit from pop songs, and so compositions that are instrumentals (like soundtracks and classical and jazz pieces) have taken a deep back seat in the process. Proponents of these types of systems argue that eventually every composition, vocal, and non-vocal will be in their system, so we should stick with it. But so far, even after over a decade of implementation, that day has not come, so if your song is not in the database, it has no fingerprint, and is therefore not showing up on what BMI and ASCAP call "surveys."

Some argue that the manpower required to actually enter all the masters into MediaGuide is more than humanly possible. So, now we're back to using some combination of metadata and watermarking/fingerprinting that hopefully fills in all the gaps.

Okay, so now, in our hypothetical, where every master has some type of software-based tracking widget in our fictional future, the next step is to have something that can identify it. Now comes the next hurdle.

2. Get every single broadcaster to put an end-user device in each of their stations that correlates this data and sends it to an independent auditor that *all three* US PROs agree is not on the take or biased in any way. Problem here: who pays for that? The broadcasters? No; they are already paying for a service to protect their interests. The PROs? If the auditor is to remain independent, then none of them can pay, or all of them must pay—like the Baseball Commissioner who is paid for by all the clubs in both US leagues. And it's clear how unbiased that seems to be for baseball. But let's say we can all agree to who the watchdog would be. Then . . .

3. After the reports come out from this auditor, have an arbitration process to ensure that every PRO and songwriter and publisher within the PRO is getting their fair slice. But who pays for this very expensive process? There are the same issues as above. Then, finally . . .

4. Have each PRO take their check back to their office and match the Music Reports info (paid for by the radio broadcasters) with the auditor's reports, paid for by (who?) . . . and then cut checks to each of their member writers and publishers.

Is this possible? Yes, with a level of intramural cooperation that has not existed in human history since the building of the Great Pyramids. And it would cost about the same as well, which would mean less money for everyone. Well, not really; it would mean less money for the people who are getting the lion's share of the money right now, but more for those who are currently receiving little or nothing. And who gets to vote on allocating the budget for this upgrade?—the people who are currently getting the lion's share of the money.

But wait. There is more fun. All the above only covers the effective collection and distribution of monies from radio broadcasters. What about film scores, both in theaters around the world and on TV? Television licensing revenues, some experts have argued, quite probably make up the majority of the PRO money. How do we make sure that the thousands of editors in the film industry—who work for producers who hate to pay for anything—fill out the cue sheets correctly? Ain't no machine on the planet that can do that. Here the honor system will always be the composer's enemy. True, you could put the same fingerprinting and watermarking technology into your scores, but that will run into problems because the music is often mixed in with sound effects and dialogue that could confuse the recognition software, leading to tangled accounting information. And this will only cover you for TV broadcasts in the US. What about theatrical use overseas, or arena uses, or industrial "needle drops," or greeting cards, or MMS (Multi-media Sending; mobile-to-mobile texting that includes multimedia such as photos, film clips, and music)?

Each of these new methods of tracking music has its own challenges for data collection. As soon as we come up with a method to conquer one, several more seem to crop up. Will we ever prevail and synchronize with Silicon Valley's seemingly ever-expanding methods of distributing our work? Probably not. It will always be an imperfect system. But at least after reading this, I hope that you'll sleep a bit easier, knowing that it's not a conspiracy to rip you off. It's just a really, really, really hard thing to do in a way that's fair to everyone.

Can I Just Stop Making Music Once I'm Signed?

Ha. Sure. How would you feel if you just invested about a million bucks in an act and they decided they didn't really want to be musicians anymore? As you can guess, record companies don't take kindly to artists changing their minds after they take their money. Most of the legal merits of whether or not you can just "quit" your deal boil down to your status under the contract. Are you an employee or a service provider/independent contractor?

Employee or Independent Contractor

In most states, the difference between an employee and an independent contractor is more than just what type of form you fill out (W4 or 1099). Just because you wish your employer didn't withhold taxes and you ask to be paid on a 1099 does not mean that the IRS will agree that you're an independent contractor instead of a full-time employee. There are specific things that constitute "employment." This is the usual standard in most states:

1. Are you in control of the quality of the product?

2. Are you using your own materials?

3. Can you leave the job any time you want?

4. Is the work performed on your premises?

If the answer to all of the above is "no," then you are an "employee" in the eyes of most states. Since the label has complete authority over the recording and distribution of your music it would seem like a slam dunk—you're an employee and are therefore entitled to benefits. So are you ready to collect? Sure, but there's a problem. The record company says you are *not* an employee. Even though you fit the legal standards above to a T, you are not entitled to any benefits, simply because the contract says "you are not an employee."

Why is this relevant to quitting the deal? Well, because status is very important if you want to try to sue the label for breach of contract; for example, if they refuse to release your record. As an *employee,* the standard for an injunction is far different and more slanted in your favor, because the law has requirements as to what an employer can do with an employee. A recording artist would be hard-pressed to sue the A&R person or producer for sexual harassment, for example, because an artist is classified not as an employee but as a "contractor," and technically should be able to walk away from the job. Sure, and give up a once-in-a-lifetime opportunity. (In 360 Deals, this is somewhat moot, since the 360 Deal by definition is a "partnership" between the label and the artist.)

So "quitting" is not as easy as you thought, since you were never "hired" in the first place. What if you just don't perform? Or what if you make annoying, demanding phone calls to the president of the label until they cut you loose? It ain't gonna work. A clause called a "negative covenant" prevents you from doing anything that disses the label or is not in the spirit of the deal.

Leaving Members

Okay, so you can't leave the label, and the label won't let you go. (Sounds like an Italian marriage.) Is there a loophole that maybe they forgot about? What if you quit the group? What if you have "creative differences"? I mean, they can't make you do business with people you hate, can they? Well, yes, they can. By most contracts, if during the total amount of time you're signed (which can easily be five to 10 years), any member gets snappy, or starts thinking he's more important than the rest of the group and bails on a session, and then refuses to jam with the rest of the group, he or she is labeled a "Leaving Member." If that Leaving Member bails, you have to immediately inform the label, at which point they have the option to end the contract for the whole group or require the remaining group members to either find a replacement quickly or keep on performing as a group but not replace the one who split. If they decide for you to go for option B, keeping the group performing minus the Leaving Member, then they still have the permanent right to bind the Leaving Member to yet another contract, this time as a solo recording artist at the same royalty rates and binding clauses as the group contract.

It makes no sense for a "Leaving Member" to be paid the same rates as the other members. Chances are that the reason a member is leaving is because he writes most of the material, or is the lead singer, or some such commodity that is not as easily replaceable. He should therefore be allowed to renegotiate his deal for market rates. Furthermore, if it's a 360 Deal, the label just got huge percentages of four individual careers instead of one act's career.

All the above has to do with what happens if one member leaves the band. But what happens if the band completely breaks up? What if everyone is going in separate directions, like Bell Biv Devoe, New Edition, The Beatles, or N.W.A.? Generally, they consider each member as a "Leaving Member."

This is no joke. The label means business. This is how they

build a stable of talent. It's the reason why some producers try to create singing groups rather than single artists. Several solo acts can emerge from one group, and the producer and the label will be tied to each one individually and collectively. Remember this if you are being asked to sign into a group. It's not *like* a marriage, it *is* a marriage. And as anyone who's been down this road can tell you, divorce is expensive. The moral of this story: Make sure that the people in your group are people you can work with for a long time, because you will be tied to them, in one way or another, forever.

Universal Trades Garbage and Love

Philosopher John Stuart Mill said, "Trade is a social act." But this motto took on a possessive twist in the wake of two lawsuits against mega-label Universal Music Group (UMG): one was by alternative trip-grunge band Garbage, and the other by hard rocker Courtney Love.

Love claimed that she was signed to a One-Deep imprint and got traded like a ball player right in the middle of her contract to another label in the Universal family that didn't have the first clue as to how to market her. She sued for a severance on the grounds that the deal exceeded California's seven-year limit on a service contract. Most recording contracts last well over seven years, so much would be at stake if Love kicked ass.

That same year, the wildly successful group Garbage filed suit against UMG, claiming that they used "strong-arm tactics" about honoring their contract. In 1994, producers Butch Vig, Doug Erikson, and Steve Markson formed Garbage with singer Shirley Manson. Manson was performing as Angelfish on Radioactive Records, another UMG imprint. She had sold barely 10,000 units on that deal, so when

Vig and Co. asked her to sing for them, it was a match. They formed Garbage and signed to Almo Sounds, founded by veteran record men Herb Alpert and Jerry Moss.[1] Moss was "keyed" into the deal[2]: as long as Moss remained with Almo, so would Garbage.

By December 2000, this was no longer the case. UMG absorbed all of Almo's assets and dismantled the label. UMG claimed that Moss was retained as a "consultant." But a consultant to what? Almo was defunct. Garbage, thinking they had a ticket out of the deal, wanted to walk with him.

However, sneaky lawyers at UMG pulled a rabbit out of the hat to get Garbage to stink up the place a bit longer. They claimed that Radioactive never released Manson from her Angelfish deal (even though they remained silent while she sold millions of records in Garbage). Under the terms of that 1992 deal, Manson could be made to perform for any UMG label for up to seven more Albums, even though the old deal was with a different band, on a different label, with different material, and over seven years ago.

UMG was hoping that, faced with the threat of losing Manson, Vig and the boys would succumb and stick around as Garbage. Instead they all banded together, and in January 2001, sued the industry giant.

Feel the Love. Smell the Garbage. And remember—trade is a social act.

---

1. Alpert and Moss, the "A" and "M" in A&M Records.
2. A "key man" clause, or "yenta clause," as I sometimes call it, is when the relationship between the two parties making a deal will exist only so long as the person who brought the parties together remains involved. It's routine between actors and large agencies, but in the music biz it's not as common.

Non-Compete: Not Working for Anyone Else

Now that the label has locked up your copyrights, image, identity, professional name, cyber rights, past history, and any future ideas that you have, they want to make sure that no one else can get at them. *Non-compete* clauses ensure that you will not sneak through the gaps in this agreement to perform for others. This clause ensures that you behave while under contract. Basically it says that during the total amount of time you are under contract, you're not allowed to perform, or do anything for anyone other than the record company, in regard to the recording and selling of your music. With one exception: you can perform on other people's records, even those on different labels, but not as a soloist or a lead singer. You can do this as long as: 1) your picture is not on the record or its packaging; and 2) your credit in the record's liner notes says you are a "sideperson," and only lists your name, and not the name of your band, unless the label gives you written approval.

This seems fairly reasonable, but what if this is not your first record deal? What if you have master recordings on some small indie, prior to you signing the new deal on a major? Or what if you're currently selling a self-made and self-distributed CD on your own and don't want to give your new major label rights to it because it's your bread and butter? Most majors will let you keep your homespun tracks as long as you agree to put them behind you to work on creating and promoting the new record. But you have to ask for this. If you don't, then you'd be in breach of contract if you continued to work on your indie recording.

Why Doesn't the Government Do Something About Piracy?

The truth is that they are doing (and have done) a great deal, when you consider their priorities. The music business ain't exactly a main concern of Congress or the White House, y'know. They have economic crises to deal with, bailouts, Wall Street corruption, environmental issues, etc., and when they get some spare time, they look at private industry concerns. When that happens they tend to prioritize based on the greatest number of people and dollars affected. The chart The chart on page 149 shows the basic breakdown of US industries. You can see that entertainment is far below some other basic needs of our complex society. If you break down entertainment further into subcategories, you see that the music business is scraping the bottom, with a mere $10 billion a year in revenue. That's about a week's worth of revenue in the oil industry.

Music does not play a role in national defense or Homeland Security, like agriculture, energy, or precious metals does. Music is a distraction for most people. Background while we do our work.

Now, having said all that, the RIAA (Recording Industry Association of America) has appeared in front of the Supreme Court and Congress more times in the past 10 years than almost all the industries above it in my chart. Why? One word: *piracy*. The RIAA's claims of lost revenue due to P2P file sharing has caught the attention of everyone. But, if music is so insignificant in the larger scheme of things, why pay so much attention to a piracy claim?

The answer is because copyrights—and more generally, intellectual property (IP)—are the backbone of almost every American industry. The concept that an idea can be owned is what creates patents, trade secrets, copyrights, and trademarks. Can you imagine a world without these things? Every invention would be open to anyone to manufacture it. Every food product from Coca-Cola to Chips Ahoy could be duplicated by anyone. Military weapons, forged on blueprints, would be available to anyone. The only way to protect your idea would be to lock it in a safe and hire a private security team. Think we have too much Big Brother stuff in our world now? Just imagine if you had no legal forum to fight for the illegal distribution of your work.

So, yes, when a measly $10 billion-a-year industry says we want songwriters and record companies to be able to control their intellectual property just like Nokia can control its patents (read: shut down illegal P2P file sharing sites), the government listens carefully. They know that if they let this slide, the next step in this slippery slope will be the recipe for Coke, the plans for the next great electric car, or the secrets of nuclear weapons. The stakes are rather high.

Unfortunately, Uncle Sam can't seem to make ISPs do what they should be doing, morally and ethically, which is assisting movie and music companies in catching the wholesale offenders: people who are hosting large hubs of illegal distribution via the Internet. ISPs used to claim that they could not catch them due to the fact that all data looks the same to their filters. This is turning out to be a false claim.

Since 2008 ISPs have begun to see greater long-term profits in positioning themselves as deliverers of content. In other words, they no longer want to be thought as "dumb pipes," like a copper phone wire with no intelligence of what it's transmitting. They now want to be recognized as very intelligent pipes, and to charge different rates for different types of data/content.

But here's the hitch. Along with this new position comes the need to be friendly with content companies—the very people they've been stabbing in the eye for about a decade. So, starting in 2009, they began to turn over the personal information of infringers to the RIAA and NMPA (National Music Publishers Association). This is the same information that they once claimed was an invasion of their users' privacy. In exchange, the RIAA agreed not to file any more lawsuits against low-grade P2P users. Since the RIAA is no longer filing such suits, the public perception is that it's open season for illegal P2P; that the RIAA lost its nerve and, according to one series of articles in a tech periodical, "grew a soul." But in fact it's just the opposite. The RIAA will be pooling its resources and only going after the largest offenders, with the ISPs now as their allies. In reality it's the ISPs who grew a soul, or more accurately, grew a desire *not* to eat their own young.

Eventually illegal P2P will all but wither away. Sure, there will always be a few sites available for the die-hards. But they will be hosted in China or other countries where firewalls are presently being erected. Accessing those sites will be difficult and eventually will be a crime.

The US government has almost nothing to do with this solution, ironically, except that the FCC wants to try to regulate Internet activity. A debate over its jurisdiction in cyberspace will be ongoing well into the next decade. So ironically, the problem of P2P piracy will be handled not through government intervention, but through the application of a far older principle — greed. Business makes strange bedfellows. ISPs and content companies will be working hand-in-hand to deliver movies and music to your devices. *Ah, what a beautiful world it will be/What a glorious time to be free*. (Donald Fagen)

The Financial Universe

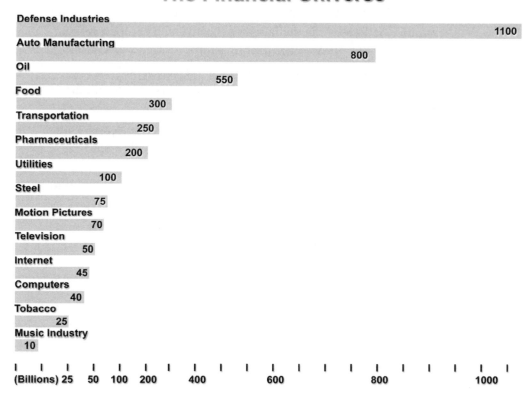

Industry	(Billions)
Defense Industries	1100
Auto Manufacturing	800
Oil	550
Food	300
Transportation	250
Pharmaceuticals	200
Utilities	100
Steel	75
Motion Pictures	70
Television	50
Internet	45
Computers	40
Tobacco	25
Music Industry	10

(Billions) 25 50 100 200 400 600 800 1000

I'm Being Hassled About Song Theft. What Can I Do?

I know, I know—this should be your biggest problem, right? You wrote a hit song and now you're being sued for stealing it. I realize that this is sort of a superstar gripe, but there are enough lessons about the business in general in the answering of it that I thought it was worth a dead tree or two (or a few microbytes, if you're reading this electronically, which there is a 1 in 3 chance that you are) to explain how this could affect even someone with no hits.

One day I was summoned to a recording studio in Hollywood to come to the aid of a client. He's a bigshot artist, so I cannot mention his name here, but he books the big old studios that he locks out for months at a time. We'll call him Sid for now. When he does this he takes over the place. Moves in his furniture, redresses the walls with his art. This is all part of his creative process. It pays off for him, too.

So I had not been to a session of his for years, and the last time he was not really a bigshot. He was on his second album. In the interim between his second album and a string of hits, Sid had become famous for several things. One of them was lawsuits where it was alleged that he had taken liberties with the co-writers of some of his material.

So on this day, when I entered the lounge of Studio A, the first thing I encountered was not Sid, but one of his assistants, who was standing outside the door to the control room. This assistant had one function. He had a stack of releases. If you've ever watched a movie being filmed on a public street, you might know what these are. If the scene they are shooting happens to grab a small piece of you walking through the shot, then they need you to "release" your rights to receive any performance royalties for "acting" in the movie. (Yes, even walking by is considered acting.) If you refuse, they cut you out or reshoot the scene.

So, this intern greeted me at Sid's door with a stack of these. Before I could go in, I had to sign a one-paragraph piece of paper that basically said, "Everything I do or say while in that room is Sid's property, and I waive all rights to it." Sound kind of extreme? It gets better. When I entered the room I did not immediately notice that Sid had several video cameras placed in strategic locations around the room. No, he wasn't making porn, or doing B-roll for his video. Sid was documenting the session. Everything that was said was memorialized. What's the point of all this? Well, Sid had been sued a few times too many for stealing songs.

It happens a lot: there is often an entourage of hang-arounders at studios. Most of the time an artist knows them personally, but as you grow in stature, you'd be surprised how strangers can creep into the outer layer of your creative sphere. Then one day you're in a meeting with your lawyer about mundane things and she brings up a suit filed against you by the studio intern, who claims that he was a co-writer on one of your songs. Or the guy delivering pizza who hung around for an hour or two to get a buzz on with the band; or an old friend who was visiting, but lately feels that you haven't shown enough respect for the old 'hood; and of course, the Ex. They all want cash and credit.

You're mortified. You know it's a bullshit claim by what is essentially an ambulance chaser, but it's going to cost you $100,000 to deal with this shit. How can you prevent this?

You never hear about these sorts of suits, mostly because record companies urge their talent to settle them very quickly and quietly. *Billboard* tends to ignore these stories because they are not good for the industry. Only when one gets out of hand does the public get wind. But for every one you hear about in the mainstream press, there are about 100 complaints that you never knew were filed.

It's very hard in a "he said/she said" situation to defend yourself without it costing you something. They say they wrote one line of a song while you were working on the demo. Do you even remember if that's true or not? How many people throw out shards of ideas in a room while you're slamming out beats? Are they all co-writers? No. Maybe, but your memory will not be enough evidence to prevent them from being an expensive nuisance.

In Sid's case his lawyer made a suggestion that most would consider too assholeish to actually pull off. He said, "Make sure everyone—everyone who enters your studio, whether you're working or not—signs a 'work for hire' release." This means that everything that they do creatively while in Sid's studio is his property.

Can you imagine inviting your buddies over to hear mixes, and when they enter you make them sign such a piece of paper? Most would leave. How about your squeeze? But

Sid does this, and he's only one of a growing number of famous artists who have begun to see themselves as targets and think it's necessary. To add extra insurance that a predator does not find a clever way around this release, he videotapes everything that goes on in the room. That way there is a record of who came up with what.

Sid is only one manifestation of a growing phenomenon in the music trade. Assistants and low-level employees and groupies see their bosses, heroes, and clients making a thousand times what they do and figure they can get a little taste if they can just convince themselves that they actually contributed in some meaningful way.

Lawyers who specialize in these kinds of cases are reminiscent of personal injury attorneys who say things like, "No, you feel bad. Here, go see my doctor and make sure you tell him how bad you feel."

Many artists carry insurance for these sorts of claims, and so the insurance company pays off. But this doesn't make the artist feel any better. Some get sued yearly and have huge premiums. And some, like Sid, are a bigger target, because if they go to court to defend themselves, as Sid did the first time, even if they win they may as well have pinned a target on their back that says, "Sue me again." Why? The perception for the next jury is that the star must be doing something wrong, because otherwise why would all these people be suing them? Sid had just had enough.

How Can I Stop Some Scab P2P Site from Distributing or BitTorrenting My Music?

Wow. This might be the stumper question of this entire book. I asked over 10 lawyers how they would deal with this. Most didn't bother to get back to me. I had to corner them at conferences and threaten to sit outside their offices with old fish if they did not tell me the secret. Then one did. He said, "Good luck trying." What he meant was that he had no answer. "You could get an injunction," he said, "but how are you going to serve it?" Many BitTorrent sites have no real brick-and-mortar offices in the US. That means US law is not prevailing upon them. An injunction will cost you a few bucks, and it might not do you any good.

Tech heads are laughing while they read this, thinking "See, these copyright people think they're so smart, but we have the last laugh." Not true. The fact that they make themselves so inaccessible and so arrogant about responding to court orders just drives home the fact that they should be shut down, and strengthens any argument made by lawyers representing content companies. As of this writing LimeWire is in danger of being shut down for thumbing its nose at the law. Despite demonstrating new business models that deter illegal P2P file sharing of music, courts don't seem willing to listen.

So the simple answer is, don't spend money trying to shut down your song on their service. They will likely be shut down on their own reasonably soon.

Reversion of Master Rights: When Is an Artist Eligible?

Every contract has a series of clauses that allow the artist to buy their way out of the deal. Maybe after you recorded your first album the A&R person was fired (or left the company). The new one who took his place could give a rat's rump about you. He didn't sign you, so if you do well it doesn't reflect on his good judgment, and if you fail, everyone will wonder why he didn't pull the plug. He may also have an artist he wants to sign that sounds a lot like you. You're now competing with others on your label who may be better connected. Or, perhaps your label merged with another one and has been told by the new upper management team to trim back the recording funds. If they had good ethics they would just release you, but labels are not known for releasing people if they can keep them without spending any extra money. Their M.O. is to hold on to you like real estate and take a "wait and see" posture. Maybe the wind will blow in a different direction in a month or two, and you'll want to come back. Maybe you'll commit suicide, causing the Master Records you did for them to suddenly be worth trillions. In this way, the label keeps you on hold while the wheels of politics and time spin. But you want to settle up and get the great recordings (finished or partially finished) that are collecting dust in the label's vault.

In almost all contracts there is a "go away" fee formula for leaving the label and getting your masters back. (Some labels call this an "exit fee" or a "parachute.") The basic equation will be something like this:

| Cost of the album you are presently recording | − | The cost of your last album

+

the cost of the album before that

÷

the number of albums recorded in both Option Periods | × | The number of unrecorded albums scheduled to be recorded in the Option Period when they let you go (usually just one) | = | The amount they will pay you to go away |

Let's plug in some realistic major label numbers. Typically each album advance is $250,000. If we use that as a base number, you often get this.

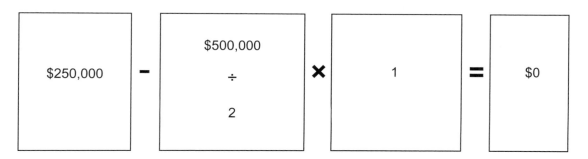

Yep. You get zero. At this point they will tell you that if you want the masters back you'll have to pay them about $250,000 for each album.

All this seems hopeless until you get to a little-known factor in the Copyright Act. Want to get your masters back for *free*? Read on.

Reversion

Some say the Mayan calendar predicts that the world will end in 2012. Even if they're wrong it seems the pop music biz will only survive one year beyond that. In 2013 many classic recordings slip out of the control of their major labels.

The hot topic at several American Bar Association conferences and music business conferences of late has been "termination of masters." Another word for that is "reversion," a little *raison d'etre* in the Copyright Act that supposedly levels the playing field for authors who are often at a disadvantage to the big, bad publisher (or record company, in this case). The Copyright Act states that after 35 years, the license or transfer of a work must "terminate" and revert back to the original author, pretty much no matter what.

Under that law's 35-year rule, artists who recorded material after January 1, 1978, are eligible to reclaim their masters beginning in 2013. If your copyrights were created/transferred in 1979, then they are eligible for reversion in 2014; if created in 1980, they are eligible in 2015; etc. From there things get a bit more complicated. Artists whose recordings are registered between 1972 and 1978 can also reclaim their masters, but have to wait a total of 56 years, starting from 1972. And if your masters were recorded before 1972, you can *never* reclaim your masters, because—believe it or not—no sound recording copyright existed before 1972. There are also narrow windows for filing the notice of intent to avail yourself of the reversion right. If you miss the window, you lose the right, and as you might guess, the length of the windows varies for each of the categories above. Ugh!

With so many variances in the law, we really need a computer to keep track of what master rights are soon to go bye-bye. (Is there an app for that?) But, due to several exceptions, the albums that are immediately affected are those released in the US from 1978–1979. So, in the year 2013, the following albums may no longer be the property of their labels:

The Wall (Pink Floyd)

Van Halen (Van Halen)

Off the Wall (Michael Jackson)

Highway to Hell (AC/DC)

Joe's Garage (Frank Zappa)

Tusk (Fleetwood Mac)

London Calling (The Clash)

Rust Never Sleeps (Neil Young)

Darkness on the Edge of Town (Bruce Springsteen)

Damn the Torpedoes (Tom Petty)

The Kids Are Alright (The Who)

Some Girls (Rolling Stones)

Fear of Music (Talking Heads)
Ricky Lee Jones (Ricky Lee Jones)
Breakfast in America (Supertramp)

Or, basically my entire vinyl collection.

As you can see, this is not an insignificant list, and this list is in *no way* complete. To make matters worse, it's not only the labels that could get the shaft here, but the artist as well. You see, *anyone* who worked on the recording is considered "an author" and can apply for a termination of their rights. ANYONE. Right down to the hanger-on who played the tambourine because he dropped off weed at the studio and someone said, "Hey, want to jam on the record?" (see the question "I'm Being Hassled for Song Theft," page 149).

Imagine being a top heritage artist. You get your masters back and you're looking forward to making a fresh deal for your classic recording, only to have the ex-entourage you left in the wake of ascension shaking you down. Even if you're legally in the right, the cost of litigation could bury you.

As a defense against this, several arguments have been put forward to further define exactly who "the author" is, but so far each one seems to have just enough merit to make the case complex and expensive to defend. The fact is, since this is the first time in recorded music history that such valuable recordings are reverting, no one knows for sure exactly who case law will decide "the author" is in this context.

For my anarchist readers, who are presently wringing their hands with glee, I'll say this: it's one thing to want labels to suffer because they're such greedy bastards. It's quite another to want to see a complete erosion of classic recordings and financial infrastructure.

Now you don't necessarily have to wait 35 years to get your masters back if you think you're stuck in a bad deal. Normally, a reversion might kick in if: 1) the label fails to commercially release the masters; or 2) an amount of time goes by (e.g., 10 years) for the label to squeeze all the profits out of the masters (which normally have a life cycle of no more than five years, unless it's a big hit). Neither of these are givens. You'll have to sue to get them back, and the label will have a series of counter-arguments that will make you think twice. But in the next section I'm going to give you some nonlegal reasons to consider when thinking about enacting your right to reversion. Here's a preview hint: Sometimes the devil you know is better than the devil you don't.

Should I Let My Record Company Keep the Rights After They Revert to Me?

This is really the bigger question. While reversion may sound like the ultimate victory for the artist, keep in mind that without the threat of label litigation, other companies would bootleg and commercially release any hit record. Can you imagine several record companies issuing Pink Floyd's *The Wall*? Each would sound the same, or maybe not. Since none have a contact with the artist, none pay royalties.

Unless the copyright administrator steps in and sues each of these parties, the work's copyright could be voided, and we will likely see a de facto public domain-ization (I made that word up) of these masters. Artistically this might be cool, because now people can do wacky remixes and P2P them free of RIAA whining, but it also means a complete deterioration of the one revenue stream that labels have been relying on for the justification it takes to invest in new artists—catalog.

Also, one has to consider that if you had a five- or eight-album deal on this label and this is only the first of the masters to enter the reversion zone, you might want to rethink how taking back those rights will affect the rest of your albums—still on that label. Will it create some animosity? Will the label believe that they are going to lose it all over the next five years and stop promoting or distributing the other albums altogether? Keeping things under one roof has often been thought to be a good strategy by industry veterans. If you agree, then the label has the upper hand in this negotiation.

So, before you get too excited about taking back those masters, consider if you have the legal infrastructure and resources to defend the copyright as well as the label that has been caring for them for the past 35 years.

But, in lieu of actual reversion, there are a number of strategies that the artist can employ to turn the situation to their advantage. In my view a clever artist would see this as an opportunity to renegotiate. Ask the label, "What value are you going to bring to the recordings from this point forward?" With Internet tools so cheaply available, you might want to point out to them that you no longer need a label to distribute your music, but you might need a partner to exploit it in new and creative ways. Ask them for a marketing plan, and make them commit to it. Or do a licensing deal or P&D deal and flip the percentages. You get 85% and they get 15%.

Bottom line: Unless you have the resources to market, promote, and most important, protect your copyrights, I would try to see reversion as an opportunity for a new deal with your label, not as a way to get away from them.

PART 5

Will Things Ever Change?

Questions and Answers from Veterans About the State of the Industry

Will They?

As stated in the book's introduction, there is no specific beginning or endpoint to this book. If you've turned directly here and you're a newcomer to the biz (under five years), then some of this will be confusing for you, because I don't slow down to explain a lot of terminology as I have in previous chapters. You need to know, for example, what ASCAP and BMI do, and if you think they are publishers, then you'll be a bit confused. But I think your turning here first also means that you're bright enough to want to know the future of the industry before you become too heavily invested.

If you're a veteran and you've turned to this section, I think you'll be very pleased at what you read here. No doubt you've become a bit disillusioned about the state of the business. You'd like to see things either revert or revolt into something more ergonomic. Either way, to quote steely Dan Quayle, who was once vice president of the United States, "The future is where most of us will be spending the rest of our lives."

Dan is right. So here goes . . .

With So Much Music Being Given Away, How Can a Producer Make Money in the Coming Years?

Producers used to get an upfront advance and points on sales, which on a successful record would generate income for many years. Now, with most records being made independently, we have a new model (which is also changing rapidly).

As income from direct sales is dropping, producers can no longer afford to think that three points on physical sales can generate enough cash to pay for the cost of production, let alone their personal bills, or god forbid, profit. And with budgets shrinking, the upfront fees are also diminishing, unless you are one of the top 10 players who can still command a six-figure fee: a shrinking commodity.

Just like record companies are looking at 360 Deals with artists, the producer needs to share in more than just sales of recorded music. The royalty structure needs to include all income the song generates, which includes airplay, film and TV syncs, and publishing revenue. There is a lot of opposition to this from songwriting societies like ASCAP and BMI, who are rightfully trying to protect their writers. But somewhere a new standard will have to emerge, or the profession will disintegrate and artists will be left to produce themselves. This may sound tempting if you're an artist who feels that labels homogenize music too much, but not to labels, especially when they see sales slumping against those acts that can afford a decent producer. Thus, labels will be looking for acts that can bring with them a known producer with a track record. This is new. In the past, the label more often than not saw themselves as the broker for such marriages. Now artists will have to hunt for themselves.

So, in the future, more than in the past, producers will be

integrated into the act. In rap, R&B, and hip-hop, this is already common, but it is rare in rock, folk, and other types of music to see producers taking on more than a creative or administrative role. Now, they will become the artist's partner in more integrated or invasive (depending on your viewpoint) ways; their deals will resemble 360 Deals, and asking for publishing, which was once thought to be the benchmark of a scumbag producer, will now become more than normal. Artists will be expected to give up something or *they* might be perceived as the sleazy ones.

I know several producers who have been co-writing with the artists they work with, and that helps to create some equity. But not all producers are (or should be) writers, although many will try their hand at it now that this new dynamic is in play. Artists who feel that the producer is doing more harm than help to the song may want to consider neutralizing the producer and offering him or her a flat cut of publishing just to shut up and stay out of the writer's corner. This does not have to include partial ownership of the copyright or a byline; just a share of income from performance royalties and licenses. Also, many producers have become studio owners, so whatever upfront fees exist, they can collect for studio time. Some studios are nothing more than a Pro Tools rig and a vocal booth, while others have real recording spaces and mixing desks.

Again, this is nothing new. Just about every producer I know owns a studio as their office, but now must begin charging separately for the use of it, whereas in the past they were bundling it into their fees.

(Thanks to Steve Addabbo for his contributions to this section.)

Why Has the Average Music Lover Happily Given Up Their CD Audio Quality for a Lousy MP3?

Hey, why did they happily give up the warmth of LPs for CDs?

Truth is, they had little choice. Whether they are happy about it or not (and I'm guessing not) music fans have had to live with more and more downgrades to the performance standard of audio for about the past 50 years. To many expert ears, compressed music files produce a thin sound compared to CDs, and certainly compared to vinyl. To compensate for this, tracks are oftentimes mastered louder. But louder is not better. Is it?

It all started with the thinning of the material of the LP. The thicker the disc, the more bass response you can squeeze out of it. But starting in the 1970s, labels opted to use thinner platters because it reduced cost, and most people didn't have sophisticated enough systems to hear the difference. Only some acts with clout were able to convince labels that their albums were worth the extra dime a copy. Mostly very successful rock and disco acts, whose sound was dependent on bass response.

It was only eight short years later that the CD made its first appearance. Many of the first commercially available CDs sounded like utter crap, because few mastering engineers at the time understood how bit conversion affected sound quality. They mastered at levels that brought the theoretical signal-to-noise ratio of 98 dB down to about 78 dB; roughly the quality of an audio cassette. And yet, when they had a choice, the public bought CDs faster than labs could manufacture them.

Around the same time, the cassette manufacturing process was going through a series of downgrades. CD copies are digitally transferred. Since it's a pure digital transfer, that means that there is no generation loss from copy to copy. It also means that each machine will receive the information exactly the same way as the previous machine. With tapes, however, the duplication process is quite different. The music is transferred to a large tape loop. This loop is put in a bin that winds the tape over the playback head very fast. As it spins, the music is transferred to many cassettes simultaneously at high speed. The faster the dubbing speed, the lower the fidelity. LPs are usually transferred at three times normal speed. This takes about a third of the high end off of the recording.

But things got worse with the advent of reverse dubbing. Instead of making a cassette in two passes—one for side A and one for side B, side A and B are dubbed at the same time. Side A is done as normal, from front to back, but side B is printed on the same tape in reverse, so that when you dub the copy, you can do both sides in one pass. Dubbing things backward created audio "ghosts" that sounded weird if you had a quality system. There was bleed through the forward audio.

There was little the buyer could do about this, because record companies wouldn't pay for slower "real-time transfers" of the album. This is why homemade "bootlegged" tapes of CDs often sounded better than the official commercial tapes, and record companies never had any issues with people making such tapes, or sharing them, as long as you bought the album first.

Yet people bought cassettes, with horrible quality and hiss, by the truckload. By 1995 CDs had gotten a lot better, and so did recording gear, moving from 16-bit to 32-bit and from 44.1 kHz to 88.2 kHz. Today, you'd be hard-pressed to make the argument that a modern recording done on quality equipment will sound better on an LP than a CD.

When MP3s hit the Internet it was due to the ease of the format. MP3s didn't sound bad because of the algorithm, but the bit rate that was chosen as a "standard" was 128 kbps. As any iTunes jockey knows, you can rip at any rate you want in AAC or MP3. Therefore, MP3s don't sound any worse than their source, unless you, the ripper, downgrade them.

It's no wonder people gravitated toward the low-grade MP3 format—at the time it was competing with muddy-sounding cassettes and poorly mastered CDs that required big boxes in order to listen to them, and that cost anywhere from $7 to $17.

MP3s were ultra-portable on those little iPod thingies, and they were free (via P2P). If you're going to have an inferior format, why not get it for free?

Those who want to blame record companies for allowing the P2P market to flourish with claims like, "If they offered buyers better quality, something they cannot get on P2P, you'd see sales recover," are forgetting about the high-quality formats—DVD Audio and SACD—that entered the marketplace the same year as iTunes went online and that died a wicked death, selling less than 500,000 in total units by 2009! (When iTunes upgraded the MP3 download standard to 256 kbps, the format became a total albatross.)

Likewise, those who stole music during the first 10 years of the new millennium with rationalizations like, "I'd pay for it if I could get what I wanted easily," were frankly lying, if you believe recent studies. Surveys of over 7,000 illegal downloaders led to these conclusions: 43% wanted music without copy protection. Period. When asked how much they would pay for a convenient legal option, over 33% said "absolutely nothing." Not a dime. Less than 15% said they would pay $1.45. And that was 1965, wLess than 15% said they would pay $1.45. And that was in a 1965 survey, when two songs, one on each side of a 45 record, cost 25 cents. That's about $1.70 in today's currency. So, buyers back then were willing to pay the modern equivalent of 85 cents a song, and the idea that music should be free would have never entered their minds. But today one in three people want to pay $0 for a song, and less than two in 10 want to pay a buck. If you think it's only students that feel this way, think again. People in this survey making more than $350,000 a year were *more* likely than poorer people to steal music.

Just as a commercial decision drove the bit rate of CDs, so too did it become the engine for iTunes' decision to offer low-grade AACs when it first launched in 2003. It would have been very difficult for iTunes to launch with high bit rates, because in the mind of Apple founder Steve Jobs, people would not want to wait more than few seconds to get the song they just paid for. Higher bit rates meant longer download time.

As cell phones and listening devices expanded in memory capacity, people who cared about audio quality began to rip at higher rates. People will likely re-rip their CDs at higher and higher bit rates as storage and bandwidth allows. I'm typing this on an iPad that has 60 gigs. I can rip at 320 kbps (three times the quality of 128k), and still get about 100 albums inside something as thin as *Time* magazine. With the next generation of memory upgrades I'll probably go lossless, or do 0% compression. I'm guessing that anyone who has the savvy to care about quality will do as I do.

And so we see that the change in sound quality is as much a reflection of our culture as it is of our technological advancements. My dad, for example, was very proud of his "Hi-Fi" from Germany. Which, in his opinion, made the best. This pride was passed down to me and my generation as well. I still have two large speakers connected to a tube Hafler amp/ preamp combination—and I built the amp from a kit. I'm a laughingstock according to my 26-year-old assistant, who doesn't understand the need for all these "room heaters." She listens to music on earbuds. And she's not alone. Since 2001, Americans have cut back spending on home stereo components by 25%; meanwhile, spending on portable digital devices has tripled.

In the coming years memory will be an insignificant obstacle, and because of the MP3/AAC formats, for the first time in recorded music history consumers can choose the quality of their favorite music. Some online music services are now marketing even higher-quality sound as a selling point. One company, HDtracks.com, has started selling downloads that surpass CDs at $2.49 a song. The future is wide open.

Why Were Major Labels So Slow/ Resistant to Respond to the Internet as a Sales Platform in the Early 2000s?

A famous historian once said, "History is an argument without end." The argument about who is to blame for the music industry's misstep regarding the Internet is only beginning. And so far only the technology side has had its turn at bat in the press, making its argument of record company narcissism and refusal to modernize. It's time someone presented the music industry's side. This is a long answer. Get a solid beverage and kick back. I'm gonna open up a can of reality that will get you mad and expose something about high-tech media and label bureaucracy that most people do not know.

A Double Standard

It is stunningly bizarre that the general public expects the record business to live up to a different standard than the other major US industries. The banking and auto industry crashes make the recorded music space's 30% tilt in CD sales since 2005 look like a gold rush. Where are the "objective" articles about how mortgage-backed-security fund managers, relying on computer-run models, should have predicted the financial crisis? (Sure, now—after the fact, after they are bankrupt—we see them.) Where are the exposés impeaching the tech geeks who persuaded the automobile execs that it's gadgets that will sell cars—not technology that makes them cheaper, cleaner, and look cool—only to watch sales drop to a 100-year low? Why aren't the mainstream journalists blaming the tech folk?

There's been not a peep. I don't think I need to do extensive research to make the obvious claim that banks and car companies spend a lot of dough on media advertising. That is what networks and newspapers survive on, and with ad revenue hitting an all-time low (also because of new technologies), no one wants to offend the few blue-chip clients that remain.

Need more examples of this dynamic? How about the travel agent industry? Why are there no articles making them out to be morons because they couldn't see that Travelocity and other travel sites would put them almost completely out of business? And then there is the porn industry, gutted by the Web: *Playboy*'s subscriptions are down 60%, from about 3,000,000 to about 1,000,000 since 2001. Sure, the video end takes a few pies in the face, but why are there no stories about Hefner Industries being foolish? Or the real estate and insurance brokerages who were all but made obsolete by Web-based forms that you can fill out to get a loan or buy insurance, even buy a car? Oh, yeah—because all those industries buy lots of ads, too.

And we need to look pretty hard to find a single dot of criticism levied at newspapers, whose entire business model was beaten into submission by bloggers and free websites. Oh right, they tend not to criticize themselves, and when we do see criticism of newspapers, it's by their competitors—TV network news.

Then there is the TV advertising industry—with revenue down about 40% since the Net came online to the general public. Why is no one calling them a bunch of foolish Luddites? Network and cable TV will soon be replaced by Web-based viewing, but no one thinks the networks are lazy and greedy for not inviting Yahoo into their offices and giving them their hard-earned catalog of shows as free content. Or the publishing industry, losing millions to Google and Amazon, which digitized books against their will. Why are they considered valiant for trying to hold their ground? Ah, well, they control the media itself, so again, we are not likely going to see anything self-critical.

Nope, to read the news it seems that only the record business consists of a bunch of greedy, nasty old white guys who just don't get the Internet. How it that? Why is that?

The fact is, *everyone* has gotten *techzonated* (my word) in the US since 2001. Everyone was blindsided by how much the Web would change things. And as recent events have shown, people who listened to the tech gurus who positioned themselves as "experts" fared no better than the ones who ignored them. But to read the *LA Times*, *New York Times*, *Wired*, et al., you'd think only the music business was shortsighted. Why?

Could it be because record companies don't buy ads, or at least not sufficiently to sway senior editors enough to think that maybe—just maybe—they should take a more fair and balanced view of the Tech vs. Content wars? In the six months that I was preparing this book I read more than a dozen pieces that indicted the entertainment industry for not embracing "advancements." Each had an "expert" talking about how the business (our business) was run by people who "just didn't understand how the Net worked" or the effect it would have. I ask you, with all this financial collapse, who did? Are we to then conclude that all these other industries whose sales have fallen through the floor or that have been completely exterminated *did* understand the Web?

"But Moses, are you saying the Internet caused the credit crisis, the financial meltdown, or the auto industry burnout?" Directly? Probably not. But swift changes are not good for large economies like ours. Smaller countries, like those in Scandinavia and parts of the Middle East, can swing a lot more smoothly than a large ocean liner like the US. Slow change allows us to grow into each adaptation, allows for people to be retrained and their skills repurposed. Fast change tends to lead to mass firings, large-scale unemployment, and recession.

What does all this macro-economics have to do with the question? Give me a few more paragraphs and I'll get there.

Imagine having to replace all the equipment in your studio in one day when you have big clients coming tomorrow. You'd never be able to connect everything, troubleshoot the problems, or assimilate the manuals, but you'd still have to let the clients in and try to wing it. We've all had to do this with that new reverb or console. Imagine having to do it with each piece of gear—all at once. Never knowing if the knob you're turning is correct until after you've screwed up the signal processing. Soon, you'd be scared to touch any knob or fader after the client says, "I love that," even if they like something you think is bad or technically wrong. Every engineer and producer out there knows exactly what I'm talking about.

Trust Was Not an Option

That, in a nutshell, using music production as an analogy, is what we are facing in the Western world due to the Internet: every piece of gear, every business concept, is now potentially obsolete, and we don't know how to integrate the new stuff fast enough to stay ahead of the client's (read: the public's) standard demands. Yet the ISPs wanted the major labels to trust them, sight unseen, in 1999. They wanted labels to sell singles over a virtual store. Major labels, being entrenched in an album-based, physical-product model that employed thousands of people and had developed a science of predicting success and failure, were naturally apprehensive.

Banks lent money against mortgages for homes that inevitably would be upside down; car companies marched forward with a "USA all the way" philosophy, unable to hear the cries of the public for a different kind of car. To say that record companies (most of which are not run by the caliber of MBAs you'll find in the banking industry) were stupid for not seeing the P2P iceberg on the horizon is nothing more than setting a ridiculous double standard.

But what made music different than travel, or insurance? Music was what ISPs wanted very, very badly. Between 1999 and 2002, Internet-based companies flooded the halls of record labels with new models for licensing deals. They didn't knock on the doors of insurance companies and say, "Give us super-duper discounts on car insurance through our website, and we'll triple your sales." They didn't do this to the travel industry, real estate, or even the porn industry, saying, "Give us free or deeply discounted stock and we'll make you more money." But they did come to the major labels with grandiose, untested ideas, wanting rights to entire catalogs for mere pennies. Why? Because everybody wants music. It's sexy.

Most were naturally turned down for reasons I'll go into in a second. Internet companies felt slighted. They retaliated by squeezing through a tiny loophole in the Copyright Act. An action that would, years and billions in lost revenue later, be legally classified as "theft."

To mask their crimes they bought their way into the public's sympathies by exploiting the bad PR labels had already accumulated over the years. They called this campaign "public awareness." They created slogans like "Information wants to be free," and "Music should be available to everyone." They sponsored "consumer rights" organizations, like the EFF (Electronic Frontier Foundation), which was and still is actually a propaganda wing for the ISP agenda and has little to do with individual rights. They bought bloggers' opinions and got them to trash the labels and got reporters to print stories about how dial-up dumb the label executives were, and how now that P2P is prolific, they are paying the price for their backward thinking. They bought huge amounts of advertising to gain the sympathies of editors who ignored the fact that the Internet was changing *everything* very rapidly and putting many businesses to the test. Instead they focused only on the devastation caused to the record business.

But the facts tell a different story. If you look at the actual numbers, instead of listening to the disgruntled, laid-off music execs interviewed by reporters who have to sell a story that their managing editor will print, you'll see that the music biz is way ahead of the curve. While industries like advertising have been all but gutted due to Internet technology, less than 10 years after Napster almost destroyed its business model, the music biz has managed to change legislation to suit many (but not all) of its copyright issues, create vast new revenue streams that have more than offset the 30% dip in CD sales, implant effective job transition (meaning trim the fat and retool with new faces) and still manage to be an $8 billion-a-year (and growing) industry in the US. ASCAP and BMI both have reported record year after year collections since 2007.

Who would have thought, in this time of crisis, when the world markets and all their tech guru advice is falling to pieces, that the music business might be the safest place to put your money?

In 2009 the music biz market cap was higher than Citibank and General Motors combined!! So how dumb are we? You don't hear us whining for a bailout. Instead we're trying to do things the right way: working with the law, pursuing licensing, and creating new avenues for income. We just don't want to give it away at a price that will hurt us. For this we are labeled as greedy. And all the media can focus on is that out of 25,000 lawsuits filed by the RIAA (less than .001% of the people actually stealing music), a few of them were adolescents and single mothers. As if the RIAA should discriminate about who is and who is not allowed to steal our work.

The IP War

The media-induced conception is that labels rested on their laurels during the advent of the Internet in the late 1990s, thus creating their own hell with illegal downloading. This is an easy pitch to buy into, especially if you have tech-related interests. It makes labels seem stupid and, combined with their reputation for not paying their artists, it's one that has been welcomed by just about everybody. But is it true? And should we care about the truth, or does it take a back seat to "justice"?

"It's not true," says Michael Ostroff, executive vice president of Business and Legal Affairs for Universal Music Group. Mr. Ostroff serves as UMG's chief legal officer, worldwide. I interviewed him in 2006 for my third book, *Million-Dollar Mistakes*, from which much of this section (with updates) is excerpted.

"It is very much a myth that record companies were saying no, no, no to the Internet," Ostroff says. "[Universal] started looking into the Internet as an opportunity in the late 1990s. One of the opportunities that we thought we would have was like the models they have in the film business. Physical product at one point, then streaming to different sources, and then buying the permanent download. Like video, pay cable, pay per view, and network broadcasts."

So, what went wrong? If labels really were reaching for this technology and the Internet companies were reaching for them, why did both sides miss the boat? Now that we're past the first-decade mark since the start of the Internet/label war, a look back might reveal, for some, an inconvenient truth.

First blood

Many tech companies approached major labels during the late 1990s for catalog licensing, but the one that seems to create the standard for examination is Napster, the David that bagged Goliath. It was the "success" of Napster that paved the way for other P2P-based companies like Kazaa and LimeWire, both of which, unlike Napster, are still operating in illegal formats.

The principals of Napster claim that they approached the majors to get the rights to legally "distribute" catalog on their P2P service as early as January 1999. Napster's perception was that labels didn't pay royalties to artists, and being very pro-artist, Napster wanted to make sure that artists were paid from their downloads (ironically). (See *All the Rave: The Rise and Fall of Shawn Fanning's Napster*, by Joseph Menn.)

But record companies faced these three obstacles in regard to licensing to online services in 1999:

➔They lacked the rights to grant.

➔They wanted to maintain the album-based business model.

➔They were afraid of anti-trust suits for imposing standardization.

While other Internet service-based companies seemed willing to engage in what must have been very frustrating negotiations with the majors, the three important factors above were obviously lost on the aggressive and naive Team Napster, whose average executive was barely 25 years old. Some execs had not even finished college. To them it seemed doubtful that these powerful labels, who could make or break careers, couldn't go boldly and quickly into something that seemed so very obvious. At least to them.

Here's how the three obstacles above broke down:

Getting the Rights Stuff. A fact glossed over by the media when criticizing record companies was that in 1999, with the exception of certain "digital rights" for jazz audiophile records, there was barely a single major label recording contract that granted artists specific rights for Internet distribution (as opposed to copies being made via a download). The now-famous broad language that we see in today's contracts that would cover any new development ("now known or hereafter invented") was not a given for heritage artists signed in the 1960s and 1970s. And even if it were, there was still a loophole that labels had to close on this issue just to protect themselves from liability. This was something labels probably did not tell the tech companies courting them for fear they would be usurped, which in fact, some tried to do. (Napster being but one.)

The crux of this problem was that some key artists

were not willing to give up their Internet rights so easily. They were still feeling the sting from years back when labels asked for the rights to re-release their masters on the compact disc (CD) format. This was a right not automatically granted in pre-1980 contracts. Throughout the 1980s, virtually every artist signed over their CD rights without receiving any upfront money. They were told instead that they would get higher royalties, because the CD would sell for about $12, instead of the usual $7.99 in 1979–80. (Artists' royalties are based on an integer of the unit price.) But after getting these rights virtually for free, labels applied a "new technology deduction" to the royalty formula, lowering payments by 25% and thus equaling the same royalty artists *already received for LPs*, which was already low, and for which transparent accounting seemed impossible.   Many artists felt duped.

Now, in the mid-1990s, less than 15 years later, the labels wanted "Internet rights"—another right not automatically granted, even in pre-1990 contracts. Even though newer artists had no choice, once-burned heritage artists with leverage balked. Many wanted an advance. Some were not interested in giving their label more rights under any circumstances, now that their contracts were in the twilight stage. And then there were the really "progressive" ones who felt that they might be able to make deals directly with Napster—laughable in retrospect but plausible at the time.

Bottom line, licensing a piecemeal catalog was considered flaccid and worthless to Napster's business model (indeed to just about every ISP-based business model), yet for labels to give Net-based entities complete catalog download rights in 1999, they would have to renegotiate with their thousands of artists. That would take years. Napster gave them about six months.

Tired of all this spit-balling about rights n' stuff, Napster forged ahead with their launch in June 1999. Artists with whom they were in direct negotiations soon backed off when they saw their own *new* releases posted on Napster's P2P network—sans authorization. It was war.

Transition from Albums to Singles. Napster was a singles-driven format—something the industry had evolved away from over the prior 20 years. Misinformation has led consumers to believe that labels loved the album format because it allowed them to package filler with the hits and charge more. This was never the case.

Labels want and have always wanted 14 hit songs on every album. Artists can rarely deliver this, and even if they can, the radio/PR format doesn't allow for too much attention to be placed on one album (with exceptions, naturally). The decision to move from singles to albums was driven by the law of averages, the economics of production, and also *by the requests of artists*.

Almost all industry advances were based on projected *album sales*. This was something artists' reps had worked for decades to achieve a standard for. Eight-album commitments were perceived as a sort of job security for many artists; with an advance based on the standard financial projections of a 14-song album and a first run of between at least 100,000 and 750,000 units.

Switching over to a singles-driven model that had little to no pressings and just a posting on a website might sound good from a consumer point of view, but this sudden change would have seriously affected the economics of just about every deal in the industry.

Articles and blogs targeting only labels in their

accusations of thickheadedness seem to want to skip over the immutable fact that songwriters and artists didn't want a "singles-driven market" either, because, if album sales are no longer the means by which you quantify success, how are you going to determine the size of an advance? What are you going to figure it against? On-demand singles?

So why doesn't *Wired* and its ilk criticize artists? Because to imply that a songwriter deserves to have his songs "shared" because he's clinging to a "dying business model" doesn't generate the same public sympathy for the tech industry. Instead, it makes them look like thugs. Better target: heartless record companies—a beard to hide the fact that stealing from majors was the same as stealing from the little songwriter too, and a great aid in helping to make illegal P2P seem victimless.

Napster didn't care to learn the economics of the music business, or how artists and songwriters pay their bills and feed their families. They just wanted the product, and they wanted it yesterday. In their mind, artists didn't get paid anyway, so why not forge ahead.

Digital Transmission Standardization. Due to antitrust concerns, there were limits to the conversations major labels could have with each other or a tech company regarding a *standard* for digital transmissions. In other words, if you as a major record company controlling a vast majority of the product make a deal with *one* tech company, you could be required to make a "most favored nations" deal with *all of them*. With several companies competing for a "standard," few media companies in 1999 were ready to do that. But you didn't read about that in most news stories. The mainstream spin was that labels couldn't adapt fast enough to keep up with the times.

If the antitrust climate that exists today had occurred even less than 100 years ago, when Union Pacific Railroad, for example, decided that they were going to create a transcontinental railroad with one type of track, every other train company would sue, claiming that Union Pacific was bullying them into conforming to an inferior standard and not allowing them to compete. We'd have railroads where you would have to change trains every 100 miles or so because train company A's trains wouldn't run on train company B's tracks.

Or, applying the same analogy to telecommunications, we would have a telephone system where you could only call people within a certain territory, because the New Jersey telephone company used a different dialing technology or a different type of cable than the ones adopted by other phone systems.

iTunes was years away, and labels, wanting to create a uniform buying experience and not get pigeonholed with an obsolete standard, asked tech companies for some rational assumptions regarding which algorithm du jour was going to prevail. No one could give assurances in 1999 other than the MP3 format, which at the time was thought by majors to be sonically inferior and did not include copy protection, like DRM.

DRM had too many technical problems for 1999 software developers. So instead of saying, "We can't figure it out," they said, "Labels are being unreasonable in their licensing demands." But another spin on this is that tech companies, by not being able to unify with a protected copy standard, forced labels to sit on their hands.

The Free Toy

In 1999 the music business had an already existing industry infrastructure, well established with standards, feeding thousands of employees and artists. The Internet "industry" was just starting out, and other than HTML, had few standards. In order for copacetic progress to happen, tech companies would need to work within the labels' existing standards. They claim that they tried, but did they really?

"I am not sure the tech companies were ever *really* reaching toward us," says Michael Ostroff. "They were interested in building a business on the back of ours *without* compensating us. [Universal was] trying to develop [its Internet] business in a more controlled manner. I think that we didn't appreciate that all of that would come tumbling down."

The rest is well documented elsewhere. Massive litigation and rewriting of copyright laws eventually closed down the free version of Napster. But by then labels had drawn blood with tech companies who simply did not understand the music industry's concerns or didn't care to. By December 1999, one month before the new millennium, a decision was made by the cabal of Silicon Valley companies: music would be the free toy at the bottom of their cereal box. Napster had proven the model.

Their PR machine in full swing, tech companies set about making record companies the bad guy in an elaborate "hearts and minds" campaign. They helped finance "advocacy groups" like the EFF, and "solutions" like Creative Commons, to "educate" the public about "fair use" and their "right to share." They seduced journalists and offered up intellectual puppets like Lawrence Lessig. And while P2P companies were losing the battle legislatively, from the public's viewpoint they gained significant ground. Just about everyone thinks only bad things about record labels. All record labels. (The average person does not distinguish between majors and indies.) The music industry missed a chance (if they ever really had one) to partner up with tech companies. Will this ever change? I think so.

The Changing Tide

Of late, ISPs have started to see themselves as content delivery service providers, instead of just "dumb pipes." Instead of "net neutrality," they now want to charge different rates for different types of content. And why not? The 21st-century commodity is not soybeans, it's bandwidth. But this requires them to make friends with their former enemies—movie and music providers. The "free toy" has become the new potential client. Time to kiss some ass.

In 2008 I was a keynote speaker at the Eurosonic/Noorderslag Conference (the SXSW of Europe). A comment in my speech was met with astonishment when I said to a room of 300 international delegates that because of the changing tide I predicted that within five years you'd see a high-profile arrest for file sharing. This seemed absurd to Europeans at the time. The Dutch government had just passed a law that made P2P practically legal. I was wrong. It would not be five years. That arrest was only a few months away in the even more progressive country of Sweden.

Since then, the US Supreme Court has upheld stiff fines from RIAA lawsuits. Britain is now penalizing file sharers, and ISPs have agreed to work with the RIAA and other special-interest groups to find and punish P2P users. Even LimeWire is on the run in federal court as of this writing. The tide is changing. The storm is clearing. When will the music biz naysayers wake up?!

Beleaguered Warner Records reported that their fourth-quarter 2009 numbers showed only a 2% drop in revenue from 2008 (adjusted for exchange rates, or what is called a "constant currency basis"). Could this be a sign? Bottom line for the future of the music biz, to paraphrase Fast Eddie Felson: "We're back!"

This is not the end. It's merely a new beginning.

With CD Sales Going into the Abyss, How Are Major Labels Staying in Business?

First, it's pure hyperbole that CD sales are going into the abyss. They are not selling as well as they did before 2005, but they are selling almost as well as they did in 1999 and 2000.

Regardless, it is something of a myth that major labels make most of their profit from CD sales. They have not since about 1992. Sure, they make income, but income is not profit. The biggest profit center for labels is the licensing of masters to film and television (and recently to new stuff like iTunes, Spotify, Pandora, etc. See the licensing section, page 89, for more on this). The cost to license content is zero, leaving a 100% profit margin. Labels get a call from a film producer or director or Internet service developer who wants a hit song in their movie, or a blanket license for a catalog. The cash register starts a-ringing. Think of the Black Sabbath song "Iron Man" in the movie *Iron Man*. What do you think Paramount paid for that license? Coupla bucks?

Back in the 1970s, when record companies made almost 100% of their money from LP sales, George Lucas licensed an entire catalog of hit songs for his low-budget film, *American Graffiti*. He paid about $75,000. Today that same negotiation would cost him about $4,000,000.

License fee negotiations for the 2008 film *Iron Man* became so steep that eventually Paramount, in an effort to save money, licensed only the underlying composition and opted to re-record their own sound-alike version with no lyrics. Rumor has suggested that this move saved them about $3,000,000 in fees.

What changed? Did faxing a contract to a film producer go up in cost 10,000% since 1971? No. What changed is that labels realized the market value of having a hit song in a film's advertising—it was key to ticket sales. They also saw that music is so much a part of our culture that screenwriters find it hard to write about anything real without stumbling into a musical reference, like a character singing a lyric in a romantic comedy. And what would the film *The Deer Hunter* be without the characters singing "I love you baby, but it's quite alright, I need you baby . . ." You get the picture.

The only film genre that seemed immune to needing to license music or music references was sci-fi and fantasy, as pop music doesn't really exist in that "world." Even so, *Star Trek* could not escape having a pop tune or two. In the 2009 incarnation, several masters were licensed to underscore situations when there usually would have been an original score. "Sabotage" by the Beastie Boys plays when Kirk is joyriding in an early part of the film.

And in the reverse, how many times have you heard the *Star Trek* theme used in other films as a parody of cheesy '60s sci-fi series, or the James Bond theme used in spoofs to underscore clandestine activity? Licenses for these placements go for many hundreds of thousands of dollars, depending on the use.

And let's not forget the granddaddy sync license of them all, the most licensed composition ever—"Happy Birthday." A song that surprisingly is not in the public domain and costs about $20,000 to have characters sing in a movie.

So in comparison, making money this way is far easier than dealing with temperamental recording artists and their issues, not to mention that there is virtually no risk on the licensing side of the business.

This does not mean that labels don't care if CDs sell. CDs and LPs were once the mainstay of label income, but when licensing began to boom in the late 1970s, record companies began to see the "disc" (the LP and later the CD) as something other than the final product.

Now the final product was the six-figure movie license, and the disc was relegated to being a way of recouping the research and development of the catalog. In other words, labels need to invest in new artists in order to build catalog that they can someday license for $1,000 on the penny. To do that, they need to spend money on creating and promoting new recordings. They need to make new hits. To recoup the cost of the development, they have the disc (and to some degree, the download). It has a manufacturing cost of about $1 and a wholesale cost of about $10. (And if it's a download it has a manufacturing cost of $0, making it a very-high-yield recoupment vehicle.)

This of course repositioned how the labels viewed artists. Once it was about creating a god for fans to swallow up. Now it was about churning out masters that would fill their catalog. Where once an artist could get more money for something like touring, to bolster the god effect, now it was easier to get a second advance to go back in the studio. (This is a major oversimplification to make a point.) Labels changed priorities as their business model evolved. 360 Deals will certainly change labels' priorities again, probably reverting back to older models (see 360 Deals, page 46).

So when labels say that most artists don't sell enough CDs to break even, they are not really telling the whole truth. Or, at least they are telling a very old truth, one that existed before the licensing boom. If by their statement they mean that an disc didn't sell enough units to recoup the artist's advance (under the ridiculous terms in their contracts), then yes, fewer than 10% of artists "break even." But if they mean that an album didn't sell enough to recoup the label's investment, then we have an entirely different picture. With this definition, about 25% of major label artists "break even" on a cost per album basis. The rest either lose money or turn a profit.

That means that when a label sells a CD for $10 wholesale to Best Buy or Wal-Mart, although they make about $6 gross, they really only make about $2 net, because the other four dollars are offsetting the losses from the other three artists that are not "breaking even." However, even this does not tell the whole story. The other three artists may not have broken even, but they probably earned something, right? They may have recouped 25% of the label's costs, maybe more. Since labels do not publicly report on their catalog derivatives, it's very hard to know what the true break-even point for a label's investment in new artists is, but we can make an educated guess that it's probably a mean average of about 50%. Meaning that for every dollar they spend on the overall development of new acts, they make about 50 cents back on disc sales. The rest has to come from licensing and other derivatives.

This may sound like they are losing cash by the truckload, but if you compare it to other industries, it's a dream. Automakers recoup about 10 cents from derivative products for every dollar they invest in the R&D of a new car, even in good times. Sometimes it takes 10 years to pay back the costs of a new model. Other industries don't fare much better. This is why the music business is so friggin' profitable. R&D is recouped at a ratio of about 1:2 with physical sales, then the hits are licensed for profits of about 10,000:1.

So that's why labels can afford a 30% drop in CD sales spread out over five years, and can still afford to pay senior execs six-figure bonuses each year. Their profit is not grounded in CD sales at all. One *Iron Man*–type license a year pays the salaries of an entire executive team. And major labels do hundreds of such licenses each year. If CD sales are down, it simply means their R&D takes a hit that year and that they cannot spend as much money on new artist development the next year (see page 88), or they have to fire a few mid-level executives until sales recover. Which history shows they always do.

Does a 30% drop in CD sales have any negative impact on the business overall? Maybe and probably, but it's not as catastrophic as the tech-biased media would have you think, nor as bad as labels would have us believe. But it is a great excuse to clean house of a few overpaid executives, drop a few barely recouped acts, and whine to Congress that we need new legislation to protect us from rampant Internet theft.

Major labels, like most big conglomerates, exaggerate to

everyone equally to serve their best interests. To artists they say "You didn't sell enough," to their staff they cry poverty in the form of a pink slip, and to the government they scream "theft."

And the band plays on.

Will the Music Business Survive Another 20 Years?

This question might be easier to answer than one would think. If we ask the question this way—"Will the music business as we know it survive the next 20 years?"—the answer is no. But if we ask the question the way it's phrased above, the answer is . . . still no, because it will survive for well over 100 years or more, and it will grow, too.

What am I talking about?

Use of the word "survive" requires only that the music business not die. Yet there is no way that the business can survive without evolution and change. Unfortunately, that does not help us answer this in a meaningful way, because one can say that about every business. This means that statements to the effect that the music business "is dying" or "will die" are rhetorical. Every business is dying if we apply the ridiculous standard that everything must stay the same forever or it is dying. As pointed out earlier in this book, once LPs were the totality of the business. Now it's physical sales, ethereal sales, and licensing. In the future it may be something else. But there will always be a demand for music, and so there will always be an entity that will furnish it for a profit, and therefore there will always be a music business.

Doom-and-gloom naysayers, brainwashed by tech-biased media stories that purport that one day soon all music will be free because copyrights are meaningless in the Internet age, are not just jaded and cynical, they are all-out stupid. Might this prediction come true in some far-off future when we have a sustainable *Star Trek* economy where people work for galactic credits? Sure. Okay, I concede that. But in our reasonable lifetime, say the next 20 years, this prediction of music business extinction is beyond impossible.

Music will always (and by "always" we mean in the foreseeable future) be worth something, and will therefore always have a value. Even if it's bundled into something else, like buying a computer or a game. If it comes inside of something, that does not mean it's free. It just means that the consumer does not feel the pinch, but believe me, there is no way Nokia or Ericsson or Microsoft is selling a phone, a game, or a PC loaded with tunes and not paying for a license for that content. When you buy *The Beatles Rock Band* for Xbox 360, you do not pay for the tracks, but they are hardly free. Microsoft paid handsomely for the rights, and about 1/10th of the money you spend on the unit goes toward that license.

The real question being asked when we ask, "Will the music business survive in 20 years?" is will there be limos and great parties like the old days, or is it gonna be a bunch of accountants? Or phrased more professionally, "Will the music biz have the power that it has enjoyed from 1962 to the present, will it have the virtual immunity from petty prosecutions that it has enjoyed?" Like when Paul McCartney was arrested in 1980 in a Japanese airport for drug possession. He was released within a few days and told never to return to the country. In less than 10 years he played a benefit concert in Japan. No jail time—in a country that normally throws the book at you for possession of a single joint. Paul got a walk because of the social equity that rock stars have aggregated over the past few decades. When we ask the question above, I believe what we are really asking is, "Will tomorrow's McCartney, whoever he may be, get the same treatment? Will music matter enough to the public to grant the industry the same kind of hall pass?" Hard to say, but you can construct your own individual basis for speculation. Then I'll give you my take at the end.

Let's think like a Wall Street commodities investor and ask

ourselves a few speculating questions that will set the parameters for our future scenarios. (C'mon, it's gonna be fun.)

1. Public Interest. Do you believe that people will take music less or more seriously in the next 20 years? And by more seriously, we mean want to collect it and assemble their own playlists, as opposed to less seriously, where people become passive and willing to listen only, and to get their music only or mostly from a radio-like environment where a man behind a curtain decides what they will hear (called "non-interactive streaming" in licensing parlance).

We also mean, will we isolate music as a listening experience separate from movies or reading, like we used to. Or will music be something we take for granted, everywhere and nowhere at the same time, like the Muzak we hear when in a mall: playing while we listen to the news or do the dishes or homework, when we're not really paying attention.

2. Commercial Demand. Will the demand for music increase or decrease? This is a slightly different question than the one above, although there is some interaction between them.

By this we mean will producers of film and TV and the public need an ever-increasing supply of material that they are willing to pay for, even if it's bundled? Will more and more establishments, like restaurants, want to pipeline music into their stores via a paid streaming service, as well as malls, offices, elevators, etc., and will the social networking conglomerates allow tools to be used to promote music, thus creating new demand?

3. Cost: Will the cost of creating new music make it viable compared to the potential profit that can be derived from the new master within a five- to 10-year exploitation period? It may cost five times less to make an album now than it did 10 years ago, but the chances of breaking even could be about five times greater too, due to the ubiquitous availability of new music. This will likely negate the cheaper cost as a positive investment factor.

To answer "decrease" or "less viable profit potential," to this question, you must believe that the chances of recouping the cost of making music masters, are reasonably close to the risk capital to create the masters. In other words , if cost for production decreases, then the risk-to-reward ratio of music also decreases. This will surely deter investors if it were to happen. The music biz of old saw ratios of 10:1 and higher.

When majors controlled the distribution pipelines, the odds were far better for them. Now labels will have to get very creative with marketing to distinguish their acts.

The syntheses of your answers to the three questions above will give you the final answer of whether there is a professional future in the making of new music and what that industry will look like. Wanna play?

Some example scenarios:

Scenario 1: Increased Commercial Demand, Decreased Cost

If the answer to question 2) above is "increased commercial demand" and the answer to 3) is "decreased cost," then the answer to 1) is irrelevant. High demand and low cost will force many new competitors into the game. In this paradigm there will certainly be a music business, but it will not be anywhere near as sexy as the one we know and love. Major labels as we know them will cease to exist because profit margins will be so slight that the space will not support their high overhead. It will be mostly small companies, meaning a few employees, and making reasonable profits is par for the course. No one is getting rich in this world, but no one is starving, either.

These small labels will be signing many, many new acts, but probably to one-off deals, a single at a time, like in the late '50s and early '60s. Advances will get lower and lower. They will be expecting the artist to do most of his or her own viral marketing, mostly though their Internet sites.

Production companies that supply new masters in this paradigm will not be a maverick producer and his entourage of hotties, like we've had through the 1990s, but an apartment or garage-size space with several computer geeks doing SEO, while a couple of others tweak and edit tracks for the various formats they are trying to market: ringtones, TV bumpers, etc.

Scenario 2: Increased Public Interest, Increased Commercial Demand, Increased Cost

If the answers above are 1) that public interest increases, but 2) demand stays the same or about the same in either direction, and 3) costs go up, then we will revert back to the heyday of yesterday's music business. Wild parties and the return of the big label and superstars that last a generation instead of six months.

Indies will all but disappear, or at best hang on by a thread, as majors drive up the cost to compete with them on a national level. Advances will get bigger, tours more extravagant (yes, they can), and musicians will once again become public icons, with opinions and the desire to run for office.

This is sort of a fantasy scenario and one that label executives dream about. If for some odd reason music became more expensive to produce but the demand for it shot through the roof, it would be boom times for majors and a death knell for indies.

For only majors would have the bankroll to supply the hungry appetite of both public and commercial demand.

I would not hold my breath for this day. If anything music is getting cheaper to produce. You can buy a 24-track production studio on the iPad for $9 that rivals anything the Rolling Stones used.

Scenario 3: Decreased Public Interest, Increased Commercial Demand, Decreased Cost

The most likely scenario, in my view. Music will find more nooks in which to be heard, but we will not notice it as much. It will become like salt — a commodity we need desperately but don't pay much for. Its cost is transparent and bundled into so many things that it feels free.

Scenario 4: Decreased Public Interest, Decreased Commercial Demand, Increased Cost

The true doomsday scenario. Catalog will reign over the market with virtually no new music being created, because why bother if it costs a ton to make and no one wants to pay for it? Since copyrights on most current catalog will be over in the next 40 years, more and more catalog will slip into the public domain (see page 15). As this happens we will see a big shrinking of the business. Far bigger than what we've seen over the past decade. Ninety percent of jobs will be slashed, leaving only copyright administration companies to haggle with each other like insurance companies in a no-fault state.

To the general public music will essentially be free. With no valuable new masters being created, the music business will deteriorate into little more than a cottage industry, until the last music publisher and label are eventually sold to an ISP who bundles the remaining bits of popular music and gives them away as value-added for opening an e-mail account or buying a new tablet.

There will be no record stores, except for used vinyl and CD stores. Record collections will become an anomaly reserved for hard-core enthusiasts who meet in secret to talk about the good old days when they saw Miles play live.

There will still be radio. Lots of it, in fact, now that they no longer have to pay anything for licenses; the stations taking on the form of cable-like genre-specific formats with automated DJs. There will be thousands of them. We will finally have commercial-free radio because almost no one will buy ads for something so ignored.

This scenario is only slightly less likely than the opposite one above it. But it's a cool bit of apocalyptic, Ayn Rand–type sci-fi that I know tech-heads who may read this will get all gooey over.

Scenario 5: Decreased Public Interest, Similar or Increased Commercial Demand, Decreased Cost

If the answer to 1) is "less public interest" and the answer to 2) is "stay about the same," and the answer to 3) is "decreased cost," then what you will have is the music industry of today. Growing in market share, but shrinking in overall size.

Right now it seems like money is slipping through our fingers, but it's not really. The same $10 billion is still in circulation. Its just that about 10% of it has been redistributed toward the bottom of the pyramid (see the illustration on page 67).

In time, as commercial demand increases and new revenue is created, this new revenue will find its way toward the top of the pyramid and it will seem like old times again, at least in terms of how much money is being made. The trade-off for this will be the glory. The glamour of the swinging music biz will be gone. As musicians we will be looked at like textile designers, and producers and record executives we will be thought of much like film or advertising executives, creative but conservative. We will have achieved respect, but given up style. We will live better, without the better life.

Sigh. Good times.

What Is The Music Biz For?

Is It Just for Making Money, or Can It Really Be a Vehicle for Social Change? Is There Anything to the 60's Idea That We Can Organize for Change Through Popular Music?

This question came to me not from a high-level music executive, but from a working musician just trying to pay bills with his art. I saved it for last and made it the sort of Afterword for this book because to me this may be the most important question asked here.

To address the question, it may be important to first understand that the pop-music business was always, by design, exploitative of its talent. This, no doubt, is what has put music's creators at odds with its investors. And when the artists and financiers of music can't seem to get along, it's not really reasonable to expect that the general pubic will see music as a galvanizing force for peace, ecology, or equal rights. I think most would agree that lately the public's enchantment with pop-music culture has lost some equity.

DRAWING BY AJA

Looking back, it's becoming harder to hold on to the image of when pop music was so strong an influence that the FBI kept close watch and files on many of its icons.

Can we get back to that place of power? Maybe. But it might not look or feel like the music business you think you know, or the one we have come to love.

Music's power vanguard was the early 1960s through the late 1970s. During that almost 30-year span, music rallied people and ultimately influenced foreign policy. It showed the world what three chords and voice can do. Unfortunately, the conditions that existed then are absent today. Mainly, portable broadcast radio as a means to experience music. Back then your favorite song was something you could hear in the background of just about any indoor or outdoor commercial space. This made music both ubiquitous and harmonious, meaning you knew that when you were hearing a socially relevant song, so were thousands of others—at exactly the same time. That was the power of radio. It unified us at a time when the draft was in effect and the youth of America was politicized.

Conversely, today we still have things to get political about, but thanks to MP3 devices and "smart radio" apps, music is now very much an *individual* experience rather than a group one. While internet technology may be revitalizing the money side of music, "iThings" have been the most significant assassins of pop's ability to be a cultural leader. We hardly turn to public forums like radio for something new, and we will never again be able to sneakily thumb through a date's record collection to get a read on their tastes or politics. Now, you'll need a password to inspect their hard drive or smart phone.

Yep, just about the only time music is uniting us face to face is, on the rare occasion, at concerts. And, according to studies, we are going to fewer of those as well. Every day, we are becoming more disconnected from music as a *social* experience and moving closer to it being a mere commodity. Pop is becoming more ethereal and more virtual, and shrinking in stature—so much so that for a few years in the early 2000s, many people thought that they had a right to *free* music because music's new virtual format felt free. Sure, stealing a CD from a record store was an obvious crime, but sharing a file? C'mon. How can that be illegal?

Will people like to own music as physical media in the future? I don't know. There seems to be no stopping the coming cloud jukebox that Silicone Valley is building. CDs will probably be the last physical medium we ever know, and yet if record labels allow physical media to disappear completely, then we will surely see the end of pop music as a cultural pavilion. Now that the group experience is absent from music, without something physical to hold, to pass back and forth to friends, there is no tactile connection to the artist or their work.

Labels are trying to hold on to the CD album standard; it means more opportunity for the artist to make a statement and more opportunity for the label to recoup their investment. It's a win-win scenario for two parties that rarely see eye to eye. But labels have been effectively neutered by an onslaught of negative press postulating that they are dinosaurs hanging on to the album format just to satisfy their own greed. As you can see, if you agree with what you're reading now, it's not that simple. Music becoming more virtual and therefore less socially relevant will surely please certain conservative powers, but it shouldn't please you. If you value music's influence on society, don't pray for the coming of the cloud. Fear it. For it is the day when an art-form that once changed a nation's view of government and war, becomes about as politically relevant as soy beans, coco, or pork bellies.

Is that the music business you want? Maybe there is an upside.

Ironically, as music loses influence it will become more profitable than ever, and not surprisingly, the people attracted to the industry will not be the most innovative. Pop music, as an art from, has become a gentrified neighborhood. Good artists and executives are still moving there, yes, but not the Picassos, Mozarts, or Einsteins. In truth, most artists I know who are successful do not think they are advancing the medium to a new level with their latest release. They don't have to record the next *Sergeant Pepper* to be happy. Nor do labels want them to, now that singles are more compatible with net-based buying habits. This is probably no big revelation.

Well, obviously if the medium of pop has run out of creative road and is conforming to the demands of Internet service providers, then in order for music to be about more than money (in other words, in order for it to be socially relevant again), then it must transform itself into something else, something for more than just a passive, private listening experience. Somehow (and I don't have the definitive answer as I write this), it must become more *interactive* between artist and audience.

I believe that we are on the verge of an essential change in the way music interposes itself in our world. In music's next incarnation, the form will be decided probably not by its creators but by its fans. Some person sitting in front of a screen IM'ing his BFF will be hit by inspiration. Someone out there reading this, maybe you, must say to him or herself, no, I'm not going to write yet another three-minute song with a verse-chorus-verse structure, not because I'm not good at it, and not because I don't think I have what it takes to make it a hit, but because the world simply does not need another one. What the world needs is for that person's unique talent for communicating to be channeled into coming up with something so different that when you first hear or see it, you cannot instantly figure out *how* it will make money. You may not even recognize it as a traditional from of pop music.

But until that day arrives, we will still be making and selling the same product that we know, over and over again. We'll find more clever ways to monetize it and re-package it. But it will only be some new version of the same old thing.

So, the answers to the questions above are yes, the music business is *just* for making money. That may not be how it started out, but that's all that's left to make of it. And no, it is not a vehicle for social change, because it may have run out of creative road, and because, more important, it's no longer a group experience. Those days are past. We can build on it. We can remold it, but we must accept pop music's destiny as a powerful medium that, like the printing press and cave drawings, is an artifact of society's youth. We need the *next* group experience. (And I don't mean Twitter.)

It's time for something new.

It's time for something new.

It's time for something *new*.

Peace.
Moses Avalon

APPENDIX

Complete List of Foreign Performing Rights Organizations

Obviously you do not have to join each one of these. Target your efforts toward where they will do the most good. But remember that big fish in small ponds get more respect. Your BMI rep may not have time to take your phone calls if you don't represent much income to them. But a small country may think a songwriter with only one hit in the US or a composer for a hot niche film is cool. They might even send out press releases and get you some free PR.

Country	Society	Full Name
Argentina	SADAIC	La Sociedad Argentina de Autores y Compositores de Música
Armenia	ARMAUTHOR	ARMAUTHOR NGO
Australia	APRA	Australasian Performing Right Association Limited
Austria	AKM	Autoren, Komponisten und Musikverleger
Barbados	COSCAP	Copyright Society of Composers, Authors and Publishers Inc.
Belgium	SABAM	Société Belge des Auteurs, Compositeurs et Editeurs
Belize	BSCAP	Belizean Society of Composers, Authors & Publishers
Bolivia	SOBODAYCOM	La Sociedad Boliviana de Autores y Compositores de Música
Bosnia/Herzegovina	SQN	Sine Qua Non
Brazil	ABRAMUS	Associação Brasileira de Música e Artes
Brazil	AMAR	Associação de Músicos Arranjadores e Regentes
Brazil	UBC	União Brasileira de Compositores
Bulgaria	MUSICAUTOR	Bulgarian Society of Authors and Composers for Performing and Mechanical Rights
Burkina Faso	BBDA	Bureau Burkinabè du Droit d'Auteur
Canada	SOCAN	Society of Composers, Authors and Music Publishers of Canada
Chile	SCD	Sociedad Chilena del Derecho de Autor
China	MCSC	Music Copyright Society of China
Colombia	SAYCO	Sociedad de Autores y Compositores de Colombia
Costa Rica	ACAM	Asociación de Compositores y Autores Musicales de Costa Rica
Croatia	HDS	Hrvatsko Drustvo Skladatelja Croatian Composers' Society
Czech Republic	OSA	Ochranny Svaz Autorsky
Denmark	KODA	Selskabet Til Forvaltning Af Internationale Komponistret-Tigheder I Denmark
Dominican Republic	SGACEDOM	Sociedad General de Autores, Compositores y Editores Dominicanos de Música, Inc.
Ecuador	SAYCE	Sociedad de Autores y Compositores Ecuatorianos

Eastern Caribbean	ECCO	Eastern Caribbean Collective Organisation for Music Rights
El Salvador	SACIM	Sociedad de Autores, Compositores e Intérpretes Musicales de El Salvador
Estonia	EAU	Eesti Atoritie Uhing
Finland	TEOSTO	Saveltajain Tekijanoikeustoi-Misto
France	SACEM	Société des Auteurs, Compositeurs et Éditeurs de Musique
Georgia	SAS	Georgian Society of Authors and Composers
Germany	GEMA	Gesellschaft Für Musikalische Aufführungs-Und Mechanische Vervielfältigungsrechte
Greece	AEPI	Societe Hellenique Pour La Protection de la Propriete Intellectuelle S.A.
Guatemala	AEI	Asociación de Autores, Editores e Intérpretes
Netherlands	BUMA	Vereniging Buma
Honduras	AACIMH	Asociación de Autores, Compositores, Intérpretes y Músicos de Honduras
Hong Kong	CASH	Composers and Authors Society of Hong Kong Ltd.
Hungary	ARTISJUS	Society Artisjus Hungarian Bureau for the Protection of Authors' Rights
Iceland	STEF	Samband Tónskálda Og Eigenda Flutningsréttar
India	IPRS	Indian Performing Rights Society
Indonesia	KCI	Yayasan Karya Cipta Indonesia
Ireland	IMRO	Irish Music Rights Organisation Limited
Israel	ACUM	Société des Auteurs, Compositeurs et Editeurs de Musique en Israel
Italy	SIAE	Società Italiana Degli Autori ed Editori
Jamaica	JACAP	Jamaica Association of Composers, Authors and Publishers Ltd.
Japan	JASRAC	Japanese Society for Rights of Authors, Composers and Publishers
Kazakhstan	KAZAK	RPA "Kazakhstan Authors Society"
Kenya	MCSK	Music Copyright Society of Kenya Limited
Korea	KOMCA	Korea Music Copyright Association
Latvia	AKKA/LAA	Copyright and Communication Consulting Agency/Latvian Copyright Agency
Lithuania	LATGA-A	Agency of Lithuanian Copyright Protection Association
Macau	MACA	Macau Association of Composers, Authors & Publishers
Macedonia	ZAMP	Musical Copyright Society (ZAMP)
Malaysia	MACP	Music Authors' Copyright Protection (MACP) Berhad
Mauritius	MASA	Mauritius Society of Authors
Mexico	SACM	Sociedad de Autores y Compositores de México, S. de G.C. de I.P.
Moldova	ASDAC	Asociatia Drepturi de Autor si Conexe din Republica Moldova
Nicaragua	NICAUTOR	Sociedad de Gestión Colectiva de Derechos de Autor y Derechos Conexos de Nicaragua
Norway	TONO	Norsk Komponistforenings Internasjonale Musikkbyra
Panama	SPAC	Sociedad Panameña de Autores y Compositores

Paraguay	APA	Autores Paraguayos Asociados
Peru	APDAYC	Asociacion Peruana de Autores y Compositores
Philippines	FILSCAP	Filipino Society of Composers, Authors and Publishers, Inc.
Poland	ZAIKS	Stowarzyszenie Autorów
Portugal	SPA	Sociedade Portuguesa de Autores
Romania	UCMR-DDA	Union of Composers and Musicologists in Romania/ Authors' Right Department
Russia	RAO	Russian Authors Society
Serbia	SOKOJ	Savez Organizacija Kompozitora Jugoslavije
Singapore	COMPASS	Composers and Authors Society of Singapore Ltd.
Slovak Republic	SOZA	Slovensky Ochranny Zväz Autorsky
Slovenia	SAZAS	Société des Compositeurs, Auteurs et Éditeurs de Slovenie
South Africa	SAMRO	Southern African Music Rights Organisation Limited
Spain	SGAE	Sociedad General de Autores y Editores
Sweden	STIM	Svenska Tonsattares Intenrationalla Musikbyra

Major Label Organization and Goals

A&R	Sales & Marketing	Promotion & Publicity	Business Affairs	Accounting & Finance	Executive
VP of A&R A&R People *(Weasels)* Asst. *Weasels*	Senior VP Marketing Dir. of Marketing & Sales Marketing Staff Sales People & Telemarketers Assistants	VP of Promotion Dir. of Promotion Local Promo Street Promoters Telemarketers Assistants	VP of Biz Affairs A&R Administration Lawyers More Lawyers Interns *(Wannabe Lawyers)*	Chief Financial Officer VP of Finance Controller Accounting Manager Bean Counters	Board of Directors Chief Executive Officer General Manager Scores of Secretaries and Executive Assistants
Product	Product	Product	Product	Product	Product
Committed artists who feel good about signing deals to create exclusive recordings the company can easily sell and don't cause too many problems	A perceived "need" for the record in the marketplace and the subsequent sale of records. This could include made-up stories about the product, sometimes called "PR."	Airplay and spins on radio stations and MTV by doing or saying (almost) *anything.* Also, coordination with indie promoters.	Well negotiated and binding contracts that protect the company's assets and limit its liabilities.	Confusing financial reports that imply profits, losses and company's financial health. Also, creating incomprehensible royalty statements.	No one really knows if they produce *anything,* but we hope and assume its policy and key decisions allow everyone else to produce their product.

Passive Revenue Streams in the Music Business

	Song (Composition)				Recording (Master)			
	Compulsory Licenses (CD sales, iTunes, etc.)	Public Performances (radio, TV, non-interactive play events)	Sheet Music & Reprints	Film & TV Placement	Record Sales (CDs, interactive play-events, ringtones, downloads)	Public Performances (non-interactive play events)	Film & TV Placement	Merchandise
Primary Middleman/ collections agency	Harry Fox	ASCAP, BMI, SESAC	Distributor	Production Company	Record Companies/ Aggregators	Sound Exchange	Production Company	Sales agents
Secondary Middleman/ collections agency	Publisher	Publisher	Publisher	Publisher	Production Company	Record Company	Record Company	Branding Company
(Manger, Financial Planner, Lawyer)								
Songwriter Composer	▢	▢	▢	▢				
Featured Performer (artist, singer, soloist)					▢	Outside of US only	▢	▢
Non-featured performer (group member)					▢	Outside of US only	▢	▢
Producer					▢			
Musician for hire					Special Payments Fund Via AFM			

ACKNOWLEDGMENTS

A book like this has many authors. Fortunately for me, I am the only one of them that gets royalties. But don't color me cocky just yet. If you take a pie-in-the-sky view and suppose that I sell 100,000 copies over the next five years, I could conceivably make about $30,000. If I divided that by the number of hours I took to put the book together, I think I'm looking at about $10 an hour; $5 after depreciation, cost of living and inflation adjustments and then... then there's taxes. (Oh, and for the books that are sold as "used" through Amazon's lovely and author-friendly, trading feature, I make $0. I want to thank Amazon for that.)

Given all that, I think I'd rather be one of the other "authors" who just wrote me an email and got a thank you below. On a time-to-money ratio, they all will do better than I and they get about the same amount of bragging rights.

As I've said publicly, as successful as my book sales have been, they barely pay for my car. But that does not mean that they are unimportant. Y'see, books live forever. Even after they are out of print, they live in people's shelves and as long as there is one copy out there, the information in them has an effect on the world. That's why writers write—not for the money but to make the world a better place. The people and places I am about to thank are all doing just that.

First, I'm going to thank some*thing*. Any writer knows that atmosphere is very important to being prolific. These are the *Silverlake* haunts where I sat with my iPad for hours at a time. I want to thank their owners for providing great food, WiFi, and a patient waitstaff while I harassed costumers into reading chapters (sometimes chasing them down the street) and took medleys of meetings and conference calls, all at considerable volume. They are: Say Cheese, Lyric Street Cafe, Bourgeois Pig, Psycobabble, and Fred 62. I'm just warning ya, I'll be back.

And now to the people. There are two types of "authors" to thank here. There are the ones who wrote in with questions and created the backbone of the book and the ones who provided insight into answers to fill out and sometimes correct my own knowledge.

Usually, I thank the industry insiders first, because they have huge egos and need to see their names before all the "little people." They can wait. This is a book of, by, and for my readers. I love and care about each of them. They are in the top five percent of great thinkers in this difficult business, and if it brings them even a simple smile to see their names here, when times can be so tough, then I am happy that I could give them that smile.

So, to my readers, many of whom I have never met but regardless took the time to write me with their questions, I say thank you. There are literally tens of thousands of you on my list and my blog, but the ones below took the extra moment to help make the world a better place through knowledge. If I left anyone out, I apologize. Sometimes an email handle was all I had to work with. And you are, in no particular order:

Matt Diedrich, Jason (Dyer) Roth, Trudee Lunden, Jeffrey Patteson, Don Van Cleave, CARA-C, Bruce Mathews, Ken Irwin, Christina Brehm, Jack Endino, Gary W. Cable, Whitney, J. "Fresh" Quintella, Aaron Wolfson, James Hurley, Rocket Japan Techmontro, Kristian Anderson, Kenneth Feldman, Margo Lenmark, Stewart Brodian, Art Toegemann, Trudee Lunden, Phil Moffa, Pamela Parker, Noemi Torres, Dr. Peter J. Wood, kushadeep, TC Smythe, Lucian Clewell, Lafe, Axel, Dan Willard, Joel Patterson, Terrell Williams, Becky Raisman, Mark Ellis, Adrian Peritore, the artist formerly known as Guy Perry, and my friend, Jimi Yamaigishei.

And to those working in this business who gave me notes and insight into my answers, you too deserve my highest appreciation. And you are (again in no particular order):

Peter Spellman, Ben Mclane, Chuck Griffiths, John Simson,

Geza X, Dan Kimpel, Steve Addabbo, Ken Freundlich, Mark Northham, Michael Morris, Michelle Shocked, Rich Ezra and my advocates, Neville and Cindy Johnson. And to all those who responded but wanted to remain anonymous, thank you for helping to make this my most informative work to date.

Finally, I am required by professional courtesy to thank my publishers and their support staff, but in truth, I would do it even if it wasn't expected; John Cerullo, Rusty Cutchin, Diane Levinson, and the entire sales staff, my pals at Hal Leonard. Thank you for your amazing promotions, support, taking me out to lunch when I come to town, and pretending you think I'm brilliant and witty.

And of course, my agent. I'd thank him or her if I had one, but in ten years of writing half a dozen books and hundreds of articles in over 50 print and web zines, the three or so that I've blown through have not managed to get me a single deal. So I want to thank them for quitting before I became a bestselling author, so I don't have to share 10% of my car.

Blessings,
Moses Avalon